GENESIS

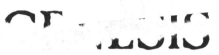

The Bibluffer's Guide

GENESIS

The Bibluffer's Guide

(Book 1 of an optimistic 66-part collection)

A comedic retelling by
PAUL KERENSA

DARTON · LONGMAN + TODD

First published in 2014 by
Darton, Longman and Todd Ltd
1 Spencer Court
140–142 Wandsworth High Street
London SW18 4JJ

ISBN 978-0-232-53075-9

A catalogue record for this book is available
from the British Library.

Designed and typeset by Judy Linard
Printed and bound in Great Britain by Bell & Bain, Glasgow

For Joseph

My firstborn, which, according to Genesis,
means he might sell this dedication to his younger
sibling for a bowl of soup.

Contents

Before the Beginning

The Bible: best-selling book of all time, and also the most shoplifted. These people think the Bible should be taken, literally.

Yet today, so many don't know what's in it. Most believers haven't read the Bible in its entirety, and most non-believers haven't got past the contents page, let alone seen the author's note or found the bit with the juggling spaniel (ssh, don't tell 'em).

So please find enclosed a rough guide to the Holy Writ's first 4 per cent: aka Genesis. I'll attempt to retell and relate via the means I know best: sketches, parodies, poems and – I'm so sorry – the occasional illustration. We should all know these stories that form part of our culture and history, whether you come to this as Bibliever or Scripturesceptic.

I don't know that the Bible is something you should just 'bluff', but if your bibliteracy is as low as mine's often been, the key stories are a good place to start. If that's you, welcome Bibluffer. Hope you learn something, or at least have a chortle at what Abraham would have been like on daytime TV. (And I know I've invented four new words in the last two paragraphs: don't worry, that's going to stop now.)

1

Start the Week

Let us begin at the beginning of the beginning...

In the beginning, when God created the Bible,
the pages were formless and blank.
Darkness was on the face of the page. Then
God said, 'Let there be words!'
And God called the words 'words', and he saw
that they were words.
And there was a header and a footer, the
first page...

...and what a first page it is: an ode to existence summarising who we are, how we got here, and why the Sunday papers are so fat. The earth begins formless, which means without any forms, which means that in a Post Office queue it would be sent to the back. Darkness is over the surface of the deep, and the Spirit of God is hoovering.

Sorry, typo on my part, I meant hovering – but yes, let's keep it in and assume there was hoovering as well. An omnipresent, omnipotent Creator was probably doing everything at once in preparation – after all, He was about to have some people round.

Day 1: So the story begins – and like any story you read, first you have to turn on the light. So God said, 'Let there be light!' And Southern Electric started charging, because the Earth was on a meter.

God could have created everything in a day, in a second, in a heartbeat. But no. In His wisdom He thought, 'I'll just do something light, like light.' Perhaps He then went for a snooze, although He kept waking up for two reasons: 1) Psalm 121 says that God doesn't sleep, and 2) He had invented light but no curtains.

So God called it a day, which was a good name for it.

Day 2: Like a hint at the Red Sea-parting to come (see next book), God said, 'Let the waters part.' Except these waters were parted above and below – to make sea, and sky. In the middle was a thing called 'the horizon', which God made slightly curved but not too curved, to puzzle humanity for some years.

Day 3: God commanded the water under the sky to be gathered to one place. And we all know that place was called 'Britain', and the time that this water did drop from the sky was called 'summer'. And when dry ground did appear, there was an instant hosepipe ban.

God called the dry ground 'land', and commanded there to be vegetation from it. And the land did listen, probably via the ears of corn that sprouted forth from the ground, which was a bit eerie. Or eary. Vegetation sprang forth all over the shop – a tree here, a shrub there. There were rainforests and meadows and grass verges and National Trust gardens that would cost twelve pounds just to look at a rhododendron and a tearoom. And God saw that they were good, although over-priced.

Day 4: At God's will, the stars and moon appeared in the sky to mark seasons and days and years, like a big calendar, except without pictures of puppies or cottages at the top. These lights illuminated the sky as a landing night-light would, and so no one did trip up on the way to the toilet at 3 a.m., but primarily because there would be two more days until people appeared to trip over things.

Day 5: God said, 'Let there be birds flying high, you know what I mean? Let there be sun in the sky, you know what I mean? And a breeze drifting on by, you know what I mean?' And there was a new dawn, a new day, a new life. And He was feeling ... good. Da dum, da dum, da dum, da da da da dum.

So God created all sea creatures, and every winged bird, and every non-winged bird, and every ostrich and penguin that has wings but more for comic effect than anything. And God looked at the living creatures and He saw they lived freely, until tomorrow, when He would create someone who might just try and eat them.

Day 6: The birds and sea creatures had a head start, but were soon put in their place (the air, and the sea) when God said, 'Let there be land creatures!' He blessed them and said, 'Be fruitful...' And the herbivores in time were full of fruit. And the carnivores in time were full of those who were full of fruit.

'...and multiply!' And the animals did work out two times two. (The idea of animals and 2x2 would come up again later.) When the animals realised what God meant by 'multiply', they set to it, especially rabbits, but pandas not so much.

Then God said, 'Let us make mankind in our image.' And mankind said, 'Hey! Who's "us"? You got someone up there with you?' And God said, 'It's a surprise. You'll find out in a few thousand years'/about thirty books' time.'

God gave mankind dominion over the animals and plants, and mankind promised to look after them, while at the same time noticing how tasty the dodos looked, and how easily the trees could be knocked down to make way for a concrete supermarket from which to sell packaged dodo.

God saw all that he had made, and it was very good. It was Friday, and creation did thank God that it was so.

Day 7: Feet up. *EastEnders* omnibus. *Songs of Praise*. *Countryfile*.

Although that implies it was Sunday, which

wasn't an official state-sanctioned day of rest until Constantine in the 300s AD. The Jewish Sabbath here is a Saturday: when work ceases, Elton John deems it alright for fighting, and Craig David starts to crave some chilling.

It was a perfect creation, with not even a couple of screws and a part H left over to which the instructions made no reference. God knew what He was doing.

THE WORLD BREWS.
And who brews it? He brews.

Who created God? I reckon He created Himself, just before the beginning – maybe at about five to beginning. All right, Psalm 90 prefers to say that God has been God from everlasting to everlasting. Potato, potarto.

The bigger challenge to the first Genesis readers was 'How many gods?' Whether you're literal (holding that Moses wrote Genesis in around 1400 BC) or liberal (we have copies of this account from about 900 BC – I say 'we', I haven't personally, not on me), this creation narrative was hitting a world of polytheists. The major stall the author is setting out is that this is all the work of One True God. Even in the basic Hebrew grammar, this is hammered home. Chapter 1's word for God is *Elohim* – which can mean God or gods – but the verbs used are definitively singular. So you could translate the opening to be:

'In the beginning... there was a God or gods... and <u>He</u> (yes, just <u>He</u>) created.'

Of course today the controversy over this bit is the big showdown of Creationists vs Evolutionists. Which of course ignores the millions in between, who might think that evolution can be created, or that creation can evolve. But no, you don't hear about them, because creatiovolutionism just sounds like a made-up word, which it is.

So let's settle this once and for all. Did God create the world in seven days? Of course not. Seven days? Are you kidding me? Seven?! Don't be ridiculous. He did it in six – see above.

2

How Do You Like
Them Apples?

Genesis is full of name-changes: Abram to Abraham (a small tweak), Jacob to Israel (only keeping one letter; a big change), Joseph to Zaphnathpaaneah (wow). But the first to be remonikered is in fact the Creator Himself.

Chapter 2 is a different story, as we zoom in on the sixth day's creation: us. (If fish had a Bible they'd probably zoom in on the fifth day's creation, and 'Jonah and the Whale' would probably be reclassified 'Some Bloke and Frank'.) God and man have the special relationship; gone – for now – is *Elohim*. Chapter 2's God is '*Yahweh*' – a personal God who walks in the garden.

My pre-schooler heard about this garden and wondered if it was like *In the Night Garden*. It's a simplistic way of looking at it, but for the CBeebies generation, yes, Addle-Paddle had a play in the Night Garden of Eden with Evesie-Daisy. Evesie-Daisy was given a Pipny-Ponk from the Pipny-Ponk tree by Snaka-Waka.

Or you might prefer a grown-up tale, like this flatshare I once heard about...

Zero Careful Owners

'I'll take it,' said Adam with glee. 'Love the garden.'

'It's nice, isn't it?' beamed the Landlord. 'I've spent a lot of time on it. Help yourself to any fruit, by the way. Except that tree.'

'What's wrong with that tree?'

'Nothing's wrong with it. In fact everything's right with it. It's just it's my tree, and they're my apples. So no scrumping. Sorry.' The Landlord sighed and leaned in. 'Listen, they're prize-winners those. I call it the "The Tree of Knowledge of Good and Evil".'

'Why do you call it that?'

'Because it gives you knowledge of good and evil.'

'Oh. Has it got pips?'

'Has it got...?' He trailed off, incredulous. 'Yes, it's got pips! I thought you might be more interested in that it gives you knowledge of good and of evil!'

'Don't like pips,' Adam replied peering back at his new room. 'What are the wardrobes like?'

'You don't have any clothes.'

'Oh yeah.'

'Hello,' Adam said cheerily down the receiver.

'Hi,' came the Landlord's tinny voice. 'It's me.'

'Oh. Is this about the damage deposit? Because I've not damaged a thing.'

'Yet. No, it was just about the "No pets" policy.'

The Landlord's words surprised him. Adam didn't

have a pet. He had a pebble he quite liked, but he didn't take it for walks or anything. 'I was thinking there was no point having such a policy. You *should* have pets.'

Adam patted the pebble on the head. 'Way ahead of you.'

'Not pebbles.' How did he know? 'Animals. I was thinking...' The voice at the end of the line sniffed and continued. '...how about every animal? You can have custody over the lot.'

'Oh. Well it's a *fairly* sizeable house, but...'

'They don't have to all stay in the house, but I'll send them past your window over the next twenty-four hours. You can give them all names. *Capeesh?*'

'That's a good name.'

'No, I meant "Do you understand?"'

'Ah,' Adam said, nodding. 'Yes, we do.'

'"*We*"?'

Adam looked affectionately at his pet pebble. 'Yeah.'

Over the next day, every animal known to man (i.e. Adam) came past Eden Cottage's front door. Adam stood in the doorway, cup of tea in hand, pointing and yelling names. 'Duck-billed platypus!' he blurted at a strange waddling creature, the words seeming to form as they left his mouth rather than in the recesses of his brain. 'Feather-tailed cockatoo!' he hurled at a low-flying bird, whom the platypus then batted away. Adam sipped his tea as the next creature hoved into view.

'This is great!' Adam exclaimed, an hour into his

marathon naming-session. 'I'm having a giant aquatic mammal of a time!' He had yet to name the whale.

Every species of penguin waddled past his door, and Adam giggled.

Fifteen hours in, Adam was struggling. 'I don't know... Aaagh!' He wracked his brain for new sounds. 'Dvark. That'll do, you're an aaghdvark.'

'*You're* an aardvark,' muttered the aardvark as it shuffled past the doorway. It turned back to look at Adam. 'And I know such insolence might see all "aardvarks" punished by removing our gift of speech or giving us weird noses, but you know what? Totally worth it.' It shuffled on towards the setting sun.

'Two minutes to go,' said the Landlord.

The rising sun's glow was slowly illuminating the Garden, where Adam sat on a log, tired hand supporting tired chin. His eyes turned to the Landlord in a weary daze, then to the parade of animals plodding past him. He sighed and waved the next few beasts through: 'Cat ... Bat ... Rat ... Gnat...'

'What happened to the big names? Where are the ring-tailed lemurs and sausage-finned hermit-tortoises?'

'They queue up early, they get the good stuff. Oh and the sausage-finned hermit-tortoise didn't last long. He was just in front of the white leopard, and ... well he was made of sausages.'

'Adam, when you've finished with this lot...'

'One second.' Adam turned to the last couple of creatures. 'Dog ... Hog ... Log...'

'No, no,' the Landlord interjected. 'The hog was the last one. You've just pointed at a log.'

'Oh,' said Adam, wiping his bleary eyes. 'Thought it was moving slowly. Come on, log!'

The Landlord rolled his eyes while Adam glared at a felled tree. 'Look, before tomorrow comes – when I'm going to have a jolly good rest – I've got someone else lined up for you. A lodger.'

'A lodger? I didn't know this was a houseshare.'

'You're going to get lonely, and there's plenty of room here.'

'Will this lodger use the wardrobe?'

'Maybe one day. Even though you and her still won't have any clothes.'

'*Her?* What do I want to live with a *her* for?! Do you think I was born yesterday?'

The Landlord checked his watch. 'Yeah, you pretty much were. Look, you've been up all day naming animals. Get some kip. You'll feel right as rain after some shut-eye. Although don't be surprised if in the morning your ribs feel a bit achy.'

'Why? Is it a lumpy mattress?' asked Adam.

The Landlord chuckled to himself as Adam's eyelids began to droop.

Adam woke the next day to hear a clatter downstairs. An intruder into his bachelor's paradise. He crept out of bed, naked as the day he was created, and nervously scratched where his bellybutton would have been. He tiptoed past the pointless wardrobe, and silently collected the inflatable novelty baseball bat, kept by the door as ironic lad kitsch. Half-asleep and halfway down the stairs, he felt his side and groaned. He pondered what he had eaten, and what that nagging thing was that the Landlord told him last night, something about a badger...

He burst through the kitchen door with an 'Aha!' and a wave of the baseball bat that would have done little to an actual burglar.

The intrudress had her back to him. 'I was thinking spices in this cupboard.' With one hand she was moving jars onto a shelf, and with the other she was binning a Pot Noodle.

'Not badger,' the man muttered, clutching his rib. 'Lodger.' He was thankful it hadn't been a *bona fide* trespasser, as he wouldn't have stood a chance.

The woman finally turned to face him. 'You're weird.'

'Madam, I'm Adam,' he announced palindromically.

'Eve,' said Eve, doing the same, extending a tin of peaches for a handshake.

Adam shook the tin of peaches, Eve realised her mistake, and they both laughed. It was the beginning of a beautiful friendship.

'Don't you go getting ideas,' Eve blushed over a cuppa. 'I mean I don't know you from...'

'Me?' Adam interrupted, and they both giggled. 'Don't worry, you can say it – "Even if you were the last man on the planet…"'

'Well, you're not,' Eve replied. 'There's the guy next door.'

'He's a snake,' said Adam, smugly adding: 'At least that's what I named him. Maybe he has other names.'

'Well, I think he's charming. He even dropped round a meal for us. You know what it's like on your first day somewhere – fridge is empty. Hope you like apple crumble.'

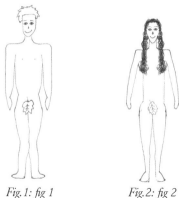

Fig.1: fig 1   *Fig.2: fig 2*

'Cream?'

'No thanks. I'm calorie counting.'

'I can count quite few looking at that crumble.' He laughed, and she joined in, until his face suddenly fell. 'Hold the phone. Where are these apples from?'

The woman rolled her eyes. 'I'm sure they're locally sourced, organically grown.' She could tell he was serious. 'They're from some tree. Gives you knowledge of good and evil or something. And I think vitamins A and C.'

'That's very local,' barked the man. 'It's from that tree out of the window!'

'Oh well, there you go. Don't need to carbon-offset any air miles.' She flooded hers with cream. Adam halted her pour.

'It's forbidden fruit. Haven't you read the tenancy agreement?'

'You're such a bloke. I bin your Pot Noodle and you shudder at the sight of one of your five-a-day.' She put the carton down and sighed. 'These agreements are never enforced. Besides, Old Snaky reckoned the Landlord just wants our mitts off it 'cos he knows we'll end up like him. Don't you want to be like the Landlord?'

'In what way?'

'I dunno. In property.'

Adam didn't like the sound of this. It was a game of Snakes and Property Ladders, and someone was bound to lose. It would probably be him again, just as he had lost earlier that evening at Strip Poker, or as they called it, Poker.

'Ah, you will, you will, you will!' Eve nudged him in the ribs, which was a sore point.

Adam eyed the pudding. His preference was Death by Chocolate, but Death by Apple was tempting. 'It does look nicely evil.'

'Or naughtily good.'

'What's the difference?'

'Wouldn't you like to know?' whispered Eve.

Adam picked up his spoon.

Eve's Recipe Book

EDEN SURPRISE

Ingredients: One apple

Serves: you right

1. *Take the apple.*
2. *Stand for several minutes to allow decision to cool down.*
3. *Using the free will, sprinkle with sin and garnish with guilt.* *C*
4. *Share apple with dinner guest.*
5. *Wait for humanity to fall, then dress with fig leaf.*

Accompaniment suggestion: Boiled snake.

C *Indicates a Calvinist option is available without the free will.*

The doorbell rang; a second later, the key was in the lock; another second and the Landlord's voice could be heard in the hallway. 'Morning! I said I wouldn't come round unannounced, so, er... Are you in?'

'I'm upstairs!' came the male lodger's voice from his bedroom.

'Me too!' came the female lodger's from hers. After a pause she added, 'I'm not decent!'

'Me neither!' yelled Adam.

'Right,' said the Landlord, still on the doormat. 'Whatever you think that means.'

'Er...' Adam's door opened a crack and two eyes appeared around it, plus a line of flesh down to the floor. Adam glanced down, suddenly aware of this, and retreated.

The Landlord summoned them. 'Would you mind a House Meeting, in the kitchen? Take your time.'

Ten minutes later, the tenants sat opposite the Landlord, both tapping nervous legs on the floor. Eve wore an apron of leaves, covering much of her body. Adam had a large fern leaf in front of his groin, plus his inflatable baseball bat for comfort.

They waited for the Landlord to speak. As he opened his mouth, one of the small fig leaves on Eve's shoulder peeled off and floated floorwards. A blushing Adam fetched the leaf and offered it back, but Eve waved the tiny leaf away. 'You keep it. You might consider it instead of that fern.'

The Landlord coughed, and the couple gave their attention.

'I'm not angry. I'm just disappointed.'

'We've let you down,' blurted Adam. 'We've let ourselves down. We've let...' He gestured his baseball bat, and it caught on a holly leaf on Eve's midriff. The inflatable swiftly exhaled and flopped onto his lap. 'We've let everyone down. I know you loved that tree.'

'It's not about the tree. It's about you listening to me. And those clothes you're wearing? Leaves?'

'...not much to the imagination, I know,' finished Adam. Eve elbowed his ribs, again causing a yelp.

'The leaves are from different trees,' Eve assured the Landlord. 'We've left the apple tree well alone.'

'I need to make sure things stay that way.'

Adam righted himself from his rib pain. 'In my defence, it was her idea.'

'Oh, thanks!' Eve exclaimed and poked him again, lightly but effectively, before turning back to the Landlord. 'It was this snake, next door. I don't know if you know him.'

'Oh I know him,' said the Landlord. 'It's more a tenancy disagreement going on there. He's ... kind of a squatter.'

'Don't know why a snake needs a three-storey house,' mumbled Adam.

'From now on, he can slither in the basement.' The Landlord leaned in. The tenants did too, as if magnetised. 'But my advice to you? Keep out of his way.' He leaned back again; the tenants stayed frozen. 'So. Where do we go from here?'

'Pub?'

'Ssh.'

'For you, my girl. I'm sorry, but you might find a bit of pain from now on, once a month.'

'Oh no!' Eve turned to Adam. 'He must be talking about the rent.'

The Landlord continued. 'Plus when you have children...'

'Now wait, we didn't deserve that!' Adam turned to Eve. 'He's going to send children to live here.'

'...that'll hurt too.'

'You're telling me,' moaned Adam. 'I've just hooked up the TV in the man-cave. Now it's got to be a nursery.'

'And your punishment, Adam...'

'More?!'

'...is no more free meals. I'm sending you to work. You hunt, you forage, and the nicest berries will be through the prickliest thorns. But come on, see it as a new challenge. From little acorns...'

Eve butted in, '...Adam can make the perfect loincloth.'

Adam took his turn to jab her in the ribs, but she didn't react, and he winced as his finger started bleeding. 'Ow! What have you been dressing with?! Is that gorse?'

'The prickliest thorns,' repeated the Landlord. 'Look, to start with, I'm giving you new clothes to wear. I brought you these.' He brought out two animal skin onesies.

Adam baulked back. 'But that's Dave! I only named him yesterday!'

'Dave?' asked the Landlord. 'What did you call him Dave for? You can't call an animal Dave.'

'You said I could name him anything I liked. And I

liked Dave. The name and the animal.' He smiled fondly at the Davesuit. 'I'll wear you with pride, Dave. And you do look comfy.'

The Landlord stood, and his tenants mirrored him respectfully. 'I'll leave you both to it for a bit. The garden's out of bounds now, of course. You've scrumped from one of my trees. I've got a Tree of Life I don't want you anywhere near.'

Eve's eyes widened. 'There's another?!' She turned to Adam. 'We could have had life! Forever! I know an apple a day's good for your health, but wow.'

'Yeah, this is exactly why I've closed the garden.'

'Fair point,' she conceded.

'But hey, there's a lot of world to see. And I'm rooting for you guys.'

The couple blushed in unison, as the Landlord strode to the front door. He turned back to them. 'When you have a kid ... I mean 'if' – I don't want to pressure you. But when you have a kid, name him Cain.' There was more blushing.

The Landlord stepped into the sun-kissed street with his first two tenants looking on from the doorstep. As he strolled away, the Landlord's fading voice could be heard: 'Of course I can set rules. But you'll think, "Yeah – I'll do what I want to do, say what I want to say, live how I want to live, play how I want to play..."'

And they did – Adam's family.

3

Brothers in 'Arm's Way

Adam and Eve set up several businesses. The farm was successful. The museum, less so – there wasn't much history about. The five-a-side football club quickly folded with only 40 per cent of a team, and actually only 20 per cent of the team really liked football.

Instead, Adam and Eve set about doubling the world's population; their sons Cain and then Abel were born. Four people in the land of Eden, for a bit...

CSI: EDEN - INCIDENT REPORT

INVESTIGATING OFFICER: D.I. Adam Gardener
INCIDENT: Homicide

VICTIM: Abel Adamson
OCCUPATION OF VICTIM: Pastoral farmer
CAUSE OF DEATH: Blunt trauma
CRIME SCENE LOCATION: Field

SUSPECT: Cain Adamson (older brother of victim)
OCCUPATION OF SUSPECT: Arable farmer

EVIDENCE: Burnt offerings from brothers Cain and Abel Adamson to the Lord. Remnants show fruit (bruised, poor quality) from Cain Adamson (suspect) and lambs (good quality) from Abel Adamson (victim).

WITNESS NAME: Eve Gardener
WITNESS STATEMENT: 'I saw Abel, my youngest, take some of his finest lambs off to sacrifice them. Half an hour later, Cain, the eldest, dragged himself out of bed and took half a punnet of old fruit out to his field. Came back two minutes later saying his burnt fruit compote didn't have any effect on the Lord. Abel though, a few hours later, came in beaming that God smiled on him. Cain didn't like that.

'There's your motive: fraternal jealousy. Next day, I heard Cain call Abel out to his field. To talk it over, I guessed. I thought Cain might ask his brother for some barbecue tips – grilling fruit to perfection, how to give a gift graciously, that sort of thing. I didn't know I'd lose a son. In many ways, I lost two.'

STATEMENT OF SUSPECT: 'All right, the fruit basket I offered God was a bit manky – it had been sat out for a few days. I kept the best for me! But Abel's barbecue was bang on, apparently. So yeah, I was peeved. Called Abel over to chat. He ran, slipped, and er, fell on a rock, I guess, I dunno, I wasn't there. I took him to A&E, or Adam and Eve as you might know them. Next thing I know I'm hauled in here by my dad thinking he's some kind of detective.

'Am I my brother's keeper? No. If he slips on some fruit peel, that's his business – like I say, it was a bit manky and easy to slip on if placed by a sharp rock.'

INVESTIGATING OFFICER'S REMARKS: I may be one hard-bitten cop, but this is the worst murder case I ever saw. The only murder case I ever saw. Hopefully the last.

'Hey sonny!' I yelled to Cain. I quit gnawing the corngrass I'd plucked from his field. The boy swaggered over, sweating guilt. I glared his way and so did the sun. All the kid could do was squint.

'So where were you four days ago at sundown?' I threw my chewed corngrass to the floor, more prop than crop.

The kid gave some half-baked story about not knowing nothing, and I reminded him that his brother had gone from Abel to UnAbel, and that I was gonna find out whodunnit.

'Whodunwhat?' he asked.

'That's my job to found out,' I told him. Figured it shouldn't take too long, only three people left on God's green earth, and I know sure as snakes is snakes it wasn't me.

Cain said, 'Maybe it was the femme fatale what done it.' His fingers nervously toyed with my discarded corngrass. He was literally clutching at straws.

I reminded the boy that the femme fatale was his own ma, and that she was with me at the time. The broad hadn't talked to him since; she couldn't. Said, 'That apple has fallen far from the tree.' And she knew a thing or two about apples, even rotten ones.

My interrogation continued under cloud, but I could see the high noon sun about to appear over our field, right over Cain's head. So I played good cop, for a second, offered him a drink a water. I looked up. The sun's rays would focus its beam as soon as the cloud passed – any second...

Now. I knocked his water to the floor. 'Don't give me any more baloney, you son of a me!' Cain shielded his eyes from the sunlight spotlight.

'Stop! Stop!'

'I'll stop when you tell me the truth! You know, I know, she knows – this is an ol' case of sacrifice envy, isn't it? It's a tale as old as time, which is about, well, a few years. You saw Cain doing well and you couldn't abide it. The younger brother! How dare he?!'

'All right, all right!' he exclaimed, his forehead sweating beads of penance. He erupted with his confession. 'It was me! In the field, with the rock. You got me bang to rights! He was the favourite, and we all knew it. So I killed him, like the fratricidal maniac I am! It's not like no one ever killed a guy before.'

'We all know that's not true,' I said to the kid. I picked some more corngrass, chewed on it, and walked away.

PLEA FOR CLEMENCY FROM MR C. ADAMSON: 'It's the first murder; I'll have to live with that. But people won't let me – they'll come after me. They'll kill me too. I'll have started a trend. I don't want to start a trend.'

CLEMENCY DEAL: Accepted. Cain to be sent east to the Land of Nod. Mark of Cain to be placed on him, to signify to any potential aggressors that he is to be untouched. Punishment on any future assailant of Cain to be sevenfold (i.e. To be sent seven times as far away? To have seven marks put upon them? To be killed seven times? ... To be clarified if it comes up).

CLOSING NOTES: Suspect known to have a new family and be building first city.

SIGNED:

D.I. Adams

33

ANTEDILUVIAN
TVTimes

7:00 p.m. Great Cities

Exile and fugitive Cain talks about building the first city of Enoch, which he named after his son. Enoch then talks about the confusion of having the same name as the place where you live, and how people address letters to simply 'Enoch, Enoch' (so good they named it twice).

8:00 p.m. Who Does He Think He Is?

Exile and fugitive Cain traces his family history. A brief show.

8:01 p.m. Horizon: The Population Explosion

An in-depth look into that age-old question: Where have all the other people suddenly come from?

4

The Generations Game

Adam and Eve had a third son, Seth. It's odd that he's lesser-known given that most biblical characters seem to be descended from him. Genesis is keen to tell us the genealogy:

- Cain's great-great-great-great-grandson Tubalcain: works in brass and iron (careful where you put that extra 's' – 'Tubalcain works in bras, and irons' means something very different).
- Tubalcain's cousin Jabal: the pioneer of tent-dwelling and cattle-farming (basically he invented 'in-tents-ive farming').
- Jabal's brother Jubal: ceaselessly plays the harp and flute.

So biblically we've reached the Iron Age, the Age of Farming Nomads, and the Age of One-Man Bands. Cain's branch of the family tree withers away, but over on brother Seth's bough you'll find a route through Noah, Abraham and King David all the way to Jesus. In fact you'd find a route to all of us. All right, the genealogists may not fully trust any family tree not accompanied by certified census documents – otherwise every episode of *Who Do You Think You Are?* would end up with the celebrity going, 'Ooh, *I'm* related to Adam and Eve too!'

Personally? I love a good story. And whether these details are exactly accurate or a few gaps have been filled in, I love the notion that I can stitch together my Ancestry.com family tree with the biblical one, whether it's bang on or not. But isn't it satisfying to just for a moment say that the route to you can be written down as easily as this?

Adam—Seth—Enosh—Kenan—Mahalel—Jared—Enoch—Methuselah—Lamech—Noah—Shem—Arphaxad—Shelah—Eber—Peleg—Reu—Serug—Nahor—Terah—Abraham—Isaac—Jacob—Judah—Perez—Zarah—Ethan—Mahol—Darda—Troes (founder of Troy)—Ilus—Laomedon—Priam—Hector (Eric Bana in Troy)—Astyanax—Polydore—Antenor—Priam II—Helenus—Diocles—Basanus the Great—Clodomir—Nicanor—Marcomir—Clodius—Antenor—Clodomir—Merodach—Cassander—Antharias—Francus (1ˢᵗ King of the Franks)—Clodius II—Marcomir III (spanned Jesus' birth)—Clodomir III—Antenor IV—Ratherious (built Rotterdam)—Odomar—Marcomir IV—Clodomir IV—Farabert—Sunno—Hideric—Bartherus—Clodius IIII—Walter—Dagobert—Genebald II—Dagobert—Clodius—Marcomir—Pharamond—Clodio—Adelbert—Wambert—Ansbertus—St Arnold (Bishop of Metz)—Ansigise—Pepin the Fat—Karl the Hammer—Pepin the Short—Charlemagne (Holy Roman Emperor)—King Pepin of Italy—King Bernard of

Italy—Pepin—Herbert I—Herbert II—Robert de Vermandois—Adele of Meaux—Ermengarde of Anjou—Judith of Brittany—Robert II of Normandy—William the Conqueror—King Henry I—Robert de Caen—Mabel of Bristol—Henry Decampernon—Oliver Champernon—Richard Champernon—Richard Champernon—Richard Champernon—Thomas Champernon—Richard Champernon—Alexander Champernon—Margaret Champernon—Robert Hill of Somerset—Giles Hill—Lady Jane Hill—Will Symes—Jane Symes— Catherine Howe of Cornwall—Joan Burnard— William Robins—Mary Robins—Mary Wills—Ann Hambly—James Rowe—Mary Hemming—Mary Sanders—Great-granddad—Granddad—Mum—Me

I say 'you'. Me. Why not now research your own family tree back to the dawn of humanity?

Historians will take issue with the above, but that doesn't affect us story-lovers. I took issue with the historicity of the singing in *Les Misérables*, but it didn't stop me humming along.

LIVE LONG AND PROSPER

The early patriarchs – Adam to Noah – didn't half go on. Living, that is. Tradition has it that most lived well into their 900s, and fathered children long after they'd received a telegram from the, er ... well, they didn't have kings then.

The Sumerian tradition (not in the Bible but in the same

era) did have kings: ten mythical, long-living kings before a Great Flood, just as the Bible has ten long-living patriarchs before Noah. Genesis doesn't tell us much about these men apart from their lifespans and their ages of procreation – and they were conceiving children at an age when they should really have known better. Whatever their untold stories are, their capers must surely sound like that old sitcom with old men (on air since Methuselah was a lad)...

Last of the Sumerian Wine
A sitcom about some very old men
and their youthful antics
(with the Bible bits in bold)

Episode **Adam** (pilot)
Adam chases **Evie** Batty around **the garden** while she hits him with assorted **fruit**.

Episode **Seth**
Crazy trio **Cain, Abel and Seth** are always getting into scrapes and **killing** each other. Hilarity ensues.

Episode **Enosh**
Enosh starts building idols. Grandma Evie Batty doesn't like it so she beats him with a rolling-pin.

Episode **Kenan**
Kenan, Clegg and Foggy get up to no good when they steal a whippet.

Episode **Mahalel**
Mahelel finds out he's expecting a son by Dinah Holmfirth, **at the relatively young age of 65**. He thinks his life's over (although **he goes on to live another 830 years**).

Episode **Jared**
Jared's famous woolly hat goes missing, just as Granddad Kenan's prize-winning whippet starts coughing up wool.

Episode **Enoch**
Enoch, Compo and Cyril go hill-walking **for his 365ᵗʰ birthday**. Compo and Cyril come back on a hot-wired mobility scooter, but tell everyone **Enoch has gone to 'walk with God'**.

Episode **Methuselah**
At the Mesopotamian Butlins, Methuselah wins the 'Have A Bottle Of Champagne Named After You' competition. The organisers offer a side-prize of a bottle a year for life, hoping he won't become **the oldest person to ever live** or anything. **Methie pops** his champagne – and **his clogs** – **at the ripe old age of 969**.

Episode **Lamech**
Lamech turns 182 and has a baby called Noah, who he teaches to swim in case it ever comes in handy.

Episode **Noah**
Old Man Noah baffles the village by taking a hundred years to build an Ark at the top of a hill. Then it all goes downhill very quickly.

5

Noah Fence

Things hit rock bottom. Eve's evil Granny Smith had spread its sin-pips far and wide, and wickedness was now growing in the spiritual orchard of planet Earth. We even hear of a race of giants – the Nephilim – who were the offspring of sons of God and daughters of men. Something had to be done, before the family trees and height differences got ridiculous.

So what do you do when your network is down? You call a helpdesk...

Calls Flood In: A Sketch

G: Hello, is anyone there? Is this a void? A firmament? An infinite loneliness?

H: Hello, Tech Helpdesk.

G: Ah, I wonder if you can help me. I've got a problem with Humanity.

H: Putting you through...

G: Fine.

      (Hold musak)

H: Hello, Humanity Helpdesk – can I take your reference number please?

G: Are you the same person?

H: Can I take your reference number please?

G: Er... 1.

H: It should be a number, a letter, then a number.

G: Oh. 3N1.

H: Just getting your details up ... Right, how can I help you today?

G: Yes, well, Humanity has gone a bit out of control.

H: Are you running Free Will 1.0?

G: Er...

H: Yes, Free Will 2.0 does fix certain bugs.

G: Does it?

H: There were compatibility issues with the Conscience app. The new version loses the Conscience app...

G: Oh, I do like the Conscience app.

H: Oh. Only we find...

G: I'm keeping the Conscience app. I just want Humanity to run a bit more smoothly.

H: What resolution are you running at?

G: 640 by several billion.

H: Have you tried uninstalling sin?

G: I don't think it's as easy as that.

H: Mmm, just checking and that would bring about a fatal error, if you did the custom install. So when did you first notice a problem?

G: Well, Temptation's been running in the background since day one.

H: Using an Apple?

G: They were.

H: Serpent virus, I bet.

G: Yes. Then Cainbot started deleting files.

H: Have you tried switching everything off and on again?

G: Well, that's what I was thinking. I'm just afraid of losing my work.

H: Ctrl+Alt+Delete?

G: I don't like to control. Or alt. Or delete.

H: It's looking like formatting the hard Earth may be your best bet.

G: Really?

H: The thing is, when you first get your Earth, it's all perfect and zips along nicely. Then gradually you install more programs, and some are great, but they don't half slow things down. Before you know it, parts are corrupted. So open up your command prompt. Have you got one of those?

G: I've got ten command prompts.

H: You need Flood.exe.

G: Okay... Will this erase everything?

H: Yes. Apart from hidden system files – you know, Mr Noah, Mrs Noah, things like that. Any Spam, Ham, Shem or Japheth. And on our website, you can download two of each animal icon as back-ups.

G: Right. And this will definitely get Humanity up and working again?

H: Well yes, but watch out for 'Babel' hackers trying

to reach your iCloud. No idea how to stop their 'Tower' program.

G: Probably disable pop-ups. Well, let's give it a go.

H: Brilliant. And if you end up at the Sod.com/com-error page, just give us a call.

(Click)

And God decided to destroy man and beast: those pesky troublemakers from creation days 5 and 6. Days 1–4 hadn't caused any problems, and the benefits of a long weekend in Creation Week now seemed apparent.

Yet one man found favour with God. So God warned this man, Noah, of the destruction to come, and sent him some instructions for an epic build, which like many building projects went on a bit.

Over 120 years, Noah's neighbours came and went, as house prices fell due to the century-long construction project. It was the Millennium Dome of its day. Surely the best hope he had was that post-completion, after years of disuse, a telecommunications company would turn it into a live music venue: the O2by2.

After years of mockery and splinters, Noah finished it. He summoned his wife and three boys – now men. Upon his instruction they ushered the animals into the ark, two-by-two, while Noah fixed the odd bit of four-by-two to the side, brought in his four-by-four.

Well, the *unclean* animals went in two-by-two. The *clean* animals went in seven-by-seven. They were designated 'clean', not because they'd been scrubbed with Radox, but because

ÄRK

ARKEA

they had been deemed suitable for sacrificing. They needed to procreate *and* provide. The unclean animals just had one job to do, the filthy swines (that's just the pigs I'm talking about – they were filthy swines).

We're told that Noah, his wife, and their sons and their wives boarded the ark. We are not told how Noah's sons met their spouses, nor indeed who was last to find that special someone...

Speed-dating with Shem

Hi! Do sit down. Right, so ... Do you like animals? No? Shame. Shem. Er, that's my name. I mean, you know that, it's on my badge. Sorry, I've never done this before. My brothers put me up to it – trying to marry me off. They're both hitched. Yeah, those ships have sailed, but this one...

Tell me about your family. Oh, mine? Well there's Mum, she's great, got the patience of a saint.

Dad's a bit eccentric. He's a builder. Well, a ship-builder. Yeah, it is a strange job this far inland, I know. Mmm, he's more on a self-employed basis.

So, er, do you keep any pets? Hamsters, great! How many? Two? Oh that's handy, Dad needs a couple of ... Where do you live again?

Me? Yeah, I'm pretty local. Down the street, hang a left, and. .. mmm, you know that house with the giant wooden construction on the drive? I know, some people get annoyed with a skip on a neighbour's drive, let alone that thing.

So this has been nice, hasn't it? Has it? Could you see yourself sailing off into the sunset with me? Oh, you get seasick. Right.

Well, all right, closing statement. Just know I'm the real catch here. These other guys are dead in the water.

Oh. No, that's fine. None taken. Let me put it another way though. What if it were up to you and me to repopulate the planet? Would you then consider a second date? Oh, okay, that sounds like a definite no.

(Bell rings)

Yep, see ya. Wouldn't want to be ya.

FACTLET: Shem's name actually means 'Name'. So it's like being called Firstname Lastname.

FACTLET 2: The Semites took their name from Shem. So if you're being antisemitic, you're being anti-Shem. And anti-'name'.

NICE WEATHER FOR DUCKS

On the 17th day of the 2nd month, it started raining. I know February can be a bit damp, but this was no light drizzle. The waters, separated on day 2 of creation week, were now reunited – the rains above and the springs below. It was the undoing of creation. The Etch A Sketch was being shaken up in a rainstorm lasting forty days and nights, like summer in a Welsh caravan park. Noah sealed his ark, and his mockers sealed their doom.

The torrents of abuse aimed at Noah now became torrents of rain. The eight people and a stinkload of animals suffered everything nature threw at them. Humanity had brought this deluge on themselves: the first example of man-made climate change.

But there was hope. Noah's family and other animals could start again, saved.

Presumably some animals got a free pass though. Sharks, for instance, may well have been for rainnihilation but survived by just swimming a bit deep. They'd stay well below the storms and old Noah, probably lying low whenever the floating zoo passed overhead. Hence their name: 'Shh! Ark.'

The rains ceased but the waters covered the land, like Kevin Costner's *Waterworld*, which is a frightening prospect. The flood lasted 150 days, which is nearly as long as Kevin Costner's *Waterworld*, which is a frightening prospect.

On the 17th day of the 7th month – so mid-July in our money – the ark came to rest on Mount Ararat in a scene reminiscent of the end of *The Italian Job*, although hopefully with less of a teetering cliffhanger. Perhaps Noah took the Michael Caine role, telling the lions and elephants to remain absolutely still so they didn't tip over: 'Don't worry lads, I've got a plan.' In many ways Noah's lot were the very first Self-Preservation Society.

On the 1st day of the 10th month, mountaintops became visible. Yet Noah didn't rush to open the doors – just because you've peeked at a peak, it doesn't mean it's time to unleash duos of chimps, emus and spaniels. You don't save them this long, only to have them drown twenty yards out of the ark.

Noah knew he needed proof that there was somewhere for them to make home, and food to eat when they got there. So...

... He released a raven: it flew off and disappeared.

... He released a dove: it flew off and came straight back.

... *He released an ostrich: it plummeted straight down with a splash, and had to be fished out by Mrs Japheth and her well-trained hippos.*

... He released the dove again: it returned with an olive branch in its mouth, *and Noah slavered at the thought of the first salad in weeks. 'And there's more where that came from!' said the dove, dropping the branch into the sea as it did so. Noah grumbled and his tummy rumbled.*

... He released the dove yet again, *saying, 'I send you out again, dove – and if you do not return then I will know you have found land!' Then mumbling, 'That'll teach you to drop my greens in the ocean.'* The dove did not return.

(Italics indicate a lack of biblical evidence for this.)

In Noah's 601st year (although he was a builder, so this may be an estimate), on the first day of the first month, dry ground could be seen beneath the mountain. It was a Happy New Year. New Year's resolutions were presumably made – mostly about taking up swimming lessons. By the end of the second month the ground was unwaterlogged and barely marshy, with only occasional sections feeling like a village fête in a Bank Holiday downpour (*'The vegetable competition must go on, Marjorie! Mr Barnett's marrows have to be seen to be believed. Wellies on!'*).

Noah and his family finally left the ark, releasing animal after animal into the wild. One or two were held back to sacrifice in grateful thanks. For them, so near and yet so far: like Jack in *Titanic* and Ernest Borgnine in *The Poseidon Adventure*, they were destined to not make the final reel of their sea voyage. In the words of Rose: 'I'll never let go' ... said just before she let go.

THE NOAHIC COVENANT

God vowed to never let go either, of humanity. From here on in, He decreed there would be no more attempts to Ctrl+Alt+Delete us. We were here to stay.

This covenant – a promise – led to several changes for us. The first rainbow was sent as an all-encompassing sign of God's vow. It would feature all of the major colours, plus indigo (which was probably there to make up the numbers – seven after all is a great biblical number. Six is rubbish).

And good news for carnivores: those sacrificial barbecues that smelt sooooo good would feature on our menu too. Before this point it was greens only, but from here on in, slam in the lamb, put some shrimps on the barbie – that béarnaise sauce was finally going to go to good use.

Possibly because of this new red meat diet, those grand ages of 600 + years each were drastically cut back, and capped at around 120. Probably for the best. No one really knows what to do with that last 400 or so years apart from jigsaws and telling the grandkids how much better it was when you were 200.

THE NOAH (HIC!) COVERED NOT

Noah retired, but had one last gift to us: wine. Well if you're suddenly allowed a nice steak for the first time, you need to wash it down with something. Alas Noah drank too much himself. It's a problem for a great achiever: boozily retelling the glory days, unable to resist an anecdote about waterproofing balsa wood and the time the camels learnt backstroke. After one such session, Noah collapsed naked on the floor of his tent.

His son Ham was the first to find him, but he didn't shield his eyes from his dad's naked form – in fact he wanted to pull his brothers in to have a laugh too. Shem and Japheth had more respect: they covered their eyes then covered their father.

(A friend of mine at uni once passed out naked and drunk on his bed. He was appalled the next morning, not by his behaviour, but by the fact that his full bin the night before had been replaced by an empty one. The cleaner never looked at me the same way again. Him. Not me. Him.)

So what does this last story teach us? Respect your parents. Don't mock drunks. And once you've seen your dad drunk and naked, that's a tough image to get out of your head.

6

A First Time for Everything

The first rainbow, the first meat-eating, the first wine-drinking … it's all happening.

We all love an origin story. Saying that, *Prometheus* wasn't as good as *Alien*. And *Monsters University* was no *Monsters Inc*. And don't even mention *Star Wars Episode 1: The Phantom Menace*.

Here though we have the original origin story. Just look at these gems, all making their debut in the Good Book's first book:

First thing	Light	1:3
First gardener	Adam	2:15
First use of a Pick Your Own orchard	Eve	3:6
First to sacrifice an animal	God	3:21
First bellybutton (with fluff)	Cain's	4:1
First to receive hand-me-down clothing (used fig-leaves)	Abel	4:2
First murderer	Cain	4:8
First murder victim	Abel	4:8

First city-planner	Cain	4:17
First musician	Jubal (flautist/harpist)	4:21
First ironworker	Tubalcain	4:22
First meat-eaters	Noah's family	9:3
First rainbow	viewed by Noah	9:13
First wine-drinker	Noah	9:20
First need for a phrasebook	Babel	11:7
First postdiluvian ruler	Nimrod	10:8
First to tithe	Abraham	14:20
First to have the Angel of the Lord appear to them	Hagar	16:7
First love mentioned	Abraham's love for his son Isaac	22:2
First circumciser	Abraham	17:23
First circumcisee	Ishmael and co	17:23
First mention of twins	Esau and Jacob	25:24
First stonemason	Jacob (built a tombstone for his wife)	35:20
First eccentrically dressed dream interpreter	Joseph	37:3
First to use a mobile phone in the UK	Ernie Wise in 1985	not in the Bible

7

The ~~Tower~~ Bar Chart of Babel

Ham's grandson Nimrod was a great hunter, and such hunty skills soon elevated him to become a great leader. But he wasn't elevated enough, so he and his people pondered how high they could go. God instructed us to go forth and spread out into the world, but Nimrod and his Babel folk had other ideas. Why explore outwards and see the world, when you can explore upwards and glimpse the next...

**Pie Chart showing Languages Spoken
in the World (pre-Babel)**

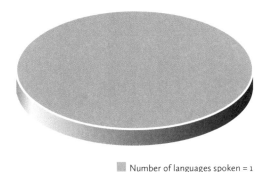

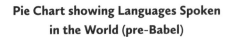
Number of languages spoken = 1

Bar chart showing how tall God would like Babel's buildings to be (where 100 = quite tall)

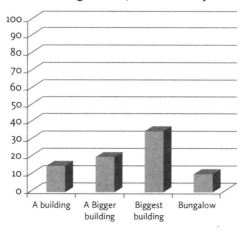

Bar chart showing how tall the people of Babel would like their buildings to be (where 100 = too tall really)

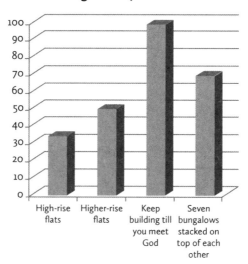

∴ **God wanted a mini, baby Babel.**

The people were elevating themselves without a firm foundation.

∴ **He invented languages!**

+ Man did get by using hand gestures + speaking loudly

+ Woman did chastise man for being embarrassing

Pie chart showing languages spoken (post-Babel) (approximate) (ie. some)

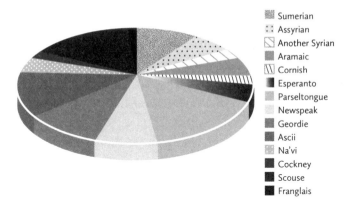

- Sumerian
- Assyrian
- Another Syrian
- Aramaic
- Cornish
- Esperanto
- Parseltongue
- Newspeak
- Geordie
- Ascii
- Na'vi
- Cockney
- Scouse
- Franglais

8
AbeTV

From here on, the book of Genesis is mostly concerned with four generations of one family:

Abraham

|

Isaac,
second son of Abraham

|

Jacob, second son of Isaac,
grandson of Abraham

|

Joseph, eleventh son of Jacob,
grandson of Isaac,
great-grandson of Abraham

At Abraham's introduction to us, he is childless, and looking like staying that way. He even has a different name – Abram. Essentially God tells seventy-five-year-old Abe and his sixty-five-year-old wife Sarai that they're going to have kids, and that he's going to add something to his name, Abe goes, 'Ha!', and God says, 'Good idea, we'll add it between the "Abra" and the "m".'

They'll need a bit of 'Abra' and indeed some 'cadabra', to produce offspring at their time of life. They're retired, settled and happy, in a place known simply as Ur. Simple folk, in a simply-named town.

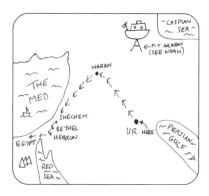

Yet God calls him, blessing his descendants. This must have come as a shock because a) they had no kids to have descendants, and b) God calling you and telling you anything is bound to a be a little out of the blue.

So at God's request, Abram and Sarai did something they never thought they'd do. They upped and left their home. They were about to become patriarch and matriarch – the reality stars of the Bible...

Now on AbeTV,  ...

| FLUFFY | SARAI | ABRAM |

FLUFFY   *Hi, I'm Fluffy McDaytime – welcome to* A Place in the Country. *One couple, one dream location, one house-move of a lifetime. This week we're with Abram and Sarai...*

SARAI   *Hi Fluffy.*

ABRAM   *Hello Miss McDaytime. I'm not going to call you Fluffy.*

FLUFFY   *So we're here in Haran. But you're after a change, Sarai?*

SARAI   *Well, neither of us is getting any younger. I just wanted to redo the kitchen. Then Abram had this calling to go to the low countries.*

FLUFFY   *Great. A 'Low Nation Location Vocation'.*

ABRAM   *Well, yes, Canaan means 'low country', so perhaps we'll end up there. We'll just follow God's will. He has promised to make us a great nation. He'll show us the way.*

FLUFFY   *So what does your dream home need to have? Room for the kids to stay?*

SARAI   *We don't have kids.*

ABRAM   *Thanks, Fluffy. Don't rub it in.*

FLUFFY   *Right, so retirement flat, low countries ... I think we're looking west. Have you thought about journeying along the Fertile Crescent?*

SARAI	*[sobs]*
ABRAM	*You had to mention 'fertile', didn't you?*
SARAI	*[sniffs] Actually we will need some rooms because we're not journeying alone.*
FLUFFY	*Okay. A lot?*
ABRAM	*Yes, that's his name.*
FLUFFY	*What?*
ABRAM	*Lot.*
SARAI	*Abram's nephew is called Lot.*
FLUFFY	*Lol.*

*

FLUFFY	*It's six months later and I've come to catch up with Abram and Sarai.*
ABRAM	*God's led us to this place called Shechem. By the great tree of Moreh.*
FLUFFY	*Well I can't see a tree, but this is where God's guided you?*
SARAI	*Oh yes. Abram built a big altar to say thank you.*
FLUFFY	*Ah, that's where the tree went.*
ABRAM	*It was a great tree.*
FLUFFY	*So you're settled?*
SARAI	*Not quite. We're off to Bethel shortly...*
ABRAM	*That's the Lord's plan for us. We'll build another altar there.*
FLUFFY	*Is there a great tree there too?*
ABRAM	*Not for long.*
FLUFFY	*Now I've got to say. I expected your Promised Land to be a bit more bountiful. It's a bit ... faminey.*
ABRAM	*Ah, but God has promised that our **descendants***

would live here. He said nothing about it being perfect straight away. So we're going to head down to Egypt for a bite to eat.

FLUFFY   Watch out for Pharaoh down there. Sarai, you're just his type.

SARAI   Oh. Er ... thanks.

FLUFFY   Well, that's all for now on A Place in the Country. Bye!

A B E TV

Coming up: The Great Mesopotamian Bake-Off ... Don't Get Done, Get Damascus ... Middle EastEnders ... Babelwatch ... Postman Patriarch... But first, let's see what Pharaoh makes of Sarai in Part One of today's big talk show...

The Jeremiah Kyle Show
Part One

KYLE

When Pharaoh's thinking 'phwoar', how far would you go to protect your wife? Welcome to today's show, I'm Jeremiah Kyle *(or Jeremiah Springer/Opradiah Winfrey/insert name of current talk show host here).* Today's guests have quite a story to tell. Please welcome Abram to the show!

CROWD CHEERS. ABE ENTERS AND SITS.

ABRAM   Thanks, hi.
KYLE   Abram, you went travelling with your missus.
            Risky business, passing through Pharaoh's
            land. We all know he likes to kill husbands and
            take their better halves.

CROWD BOOS.

ABRAM   That's right, Jeremiah. So I told her to say she's
            my sister.
KYLE   Something we've seen on this show a lot over
            the years.
ABRAM   No, she's not actually my sister. Well, she is my
            half-sister, but the point is...
KYLE   Let's bring her out – please welcome Sarai to
            the show!

CROWD CHEERS. SARAI ENTERS AND SITS.

SARAI   Hi Jeremiah. Love the show.
KYLE   Thanks. So how did you feel being introduced
            to Pharaoh by your husband as his sister?
SARAI   I could see the point. I thought if Pharaoh takes
            a liking to me, he'll treat us well. Compared
            with him killing my husband so he can have me
            to himself, I think it was the best option.
KYLE   Well, let's see if Pharaoh liked having the wool

pulled over his eyes. Please welcome Pharaoh to the show!

CROWD BOOS. PHARAOH ENTERS AND SITS.

PHARAOH Yes, yes. Boo to you too. This my throne?

KYLE Pharaoh. Your Highness. Thanks for coming on the show.

PHARAOH Oh there they are. Brother and sister, husband and wife. Their 'Promised Land' ran out of food, so they came running to yours truly – I gave them food, livestock, servants. You can't say Pharaoh than that.

CROWD BOOS.

PHARAOH Look, I flirted a little with this Sarai woman, without a Cairo 'n the world. 'Nile tell you this: it made me very unhappyr amid all this. I don't care what anyone sphinx – 'E jipped me!

KYLE Eh?

PHARAOH 'Egypt'. I could have killed him. But I didn't. I said, 'Hi rogue, live!'

ABRAM You what?

PHARAOH   'Hieroglyph', keep up. But I'm still furious with them!

KYLE   How furious, Pharaoh? Furious enough ... to throw a chair?

PHARAOH   Certainly not. I have people to do that for me. Guards!

KYLE   Get him out of here!

PHARAOH IS DRAGGED OFF STAGE.

KYLE   Abram, we've got someone else you fell out with. Please welcome Lot to the show!

CROWD CHEERS. LOT ENTERS AND SITS.

LOT   Hello Uncle Abe. Auntie Sar. Jeremiah.

KYLE   That's your Lot. So, Uncle Abram divided up land with you, and you settled near Sodom and Gomorrah...

LOT   Pre-brimstone.

KYLE   Pre-brimstone. Then it all got a bit warry.

LOT   Yeah. On my new doorstep there was King Amraphel of Shinar, and he said that King Arioch of Ellasar had a big head, and King Chedorlaomer of Elam was like, 'Are you talking 'bout me?' And King Amraphel was like, 'Whatevs, I was talking to Arioch.' And King Tidal then stepped in and was giving it all like, 'Leave it lads, we've all had a drink.' And then they all made up 'cos then King Bera of Sodom came up to them, and they thought he was looking at one of their birds funny, which was quite unlikely, but I don't care or nothing.

KYLE   Right, and where do you fit into this, Lot?

LOT   Well, then like it all kicked off in the car park of Siddim, and I was bundled into this Escort and someone shoved me in a lock-up.

KYLE   And word got to your Uncle Abram about this trouble you'd been getting into, Lot?

LOT   It weren't my trouble! I was in the wrong place at the wrong time! But yeah, Unc got tooled up, snuck in and sorted out them guys what was left. He was well nifty for an old codger.

ABRAM   Thanks, nephew.

LOT   Whevs.

KYLE   More from us later. Now let's go to commercial...

Abevert 1:   **Do you like bread? How about some wine? Then you'll love 'Free Bread and Wine'. Locally sourced from local priest and king Melchizedek, it's the**

perfect post-war pick-me-up if your name's Abram. Apply now and as a free gift you'll also get some foreshadowing of Jesus' Last Supper in the New Testament.

Abevert 2   Have you thought of tithing? Then why not try it?! It's all the rage! If you've been offered bread and wine by a local priest and king, then tithing is the perfect way to say, 'Cheers!' All you need to do is give ten per cent – that's right, just ten per cent of your income, and your tithing's done!**

**10 per cent tithe typical APR. Tithing may vary by approx 0 per cent. Your home is not at risk if you do not keep up repayments.

Now on AbeTV, Abram meets his maker, who puts him into a deep sleep. (This episode contains references to circumcision.)

Scene. A patient's bed.

ANAESTHETIST: Mr Terahson? Or can I call you Abr... (coughs) ahem?
ABRAM: Abram, that's me.
ANAESTHETIST: I prefer Abraham. Let's just change that in your notes.

ABRAHAM: Eh? What kind of hospital is this?
ANAESTHETIST: Oh, it's not a hospital. Now Abraham, I'm just going to put you into a little sleep.
ABRAHAM: What? Why?
ANAESTHETIST: Because I am the Lord your God.
ABRAHAM: Oh. Right.
ANAESTHETIST: Ssh. Don't tell the staff. So I've got a couple of visions to show you, of how life in the Promised Land won't be easy, how your descendants will firstly live in a strange land where they'll serve the kingdom before being released. But nothing to worry about. Any questions?
ABRAHAM: Actually one while you're here. You keep talking about my descendants...
ANAESTHETIST: Oh yes, look to your left, out of that window at the night sky. The number of stars you see, that's the number of your descendants.
ABRAHAM: (turns right) Wow. None?
ANAESTHETIST: That's the black screen we put around the beds.
ABRAHAM: (turns left) Ooh. Lots of stars. So how am I going to have descendants when my wife and I have no kids?
ANAESTHETIST: You are a man of great faith, Abraham.
ABRAHAM: And great patience.
ANAESTHETIST: You will have a child. 'He that shall come forth out of thine own bowels, he shall

66

be thine heir!'

ABRAHAM: My bowels? Are you sure?

ANAESTHETIST: It's a figure of speech.

ABRAHAM: Well, wherever they're coming from, it's great news. Can't wait to tell Sarai. Although I might leave out the bit about the bowels.

ANAESTHETIST: Ah, I have autocorrected her name to Sarah.

ABRAHAM: Oh, righto. Anyone else? What's Lot called? He could really do with a name-change.

ANAESTHETIST: He's called Lot. One other thing. This covenant we have, this contract ... I want you to cut something.

ABRAHAM: Which clause?

ANAESTHETIST: Well no, not a clause.

ABRAHAM: Cut what then? You'll have to excuse my weak brain - I'm fourscore years and six...

ANAESTHETIST: Yes. There. You said it. Nearly.

ABRAHAM: Fourscore?

ANAESTHETIST: Foreskin. As a symbol of the covenant.

ABRAHAM: A symbol? Couldn't I just wear a badge?

ANAESTHETIST: Yes you can. A badge of your foreskin.

ABRAHAM: And you're going to do the cutting when you've put me to sleep?

ANAESTHETIST: Er, no, I'm just going to show you those visions. You circumcise on your own time.

ABRAHAM: And I'm definitely going to have kids?

	Even though you're asking me to start cutting bits off?
ANAESTHETIST:	Yep. Oh, and just do the same to all the men in your household, and any boys born, around the eight-day mark.
ABRAHAM:	And you think my staff will do this willingly?
ANAESTHETIST:	Say you're making some cuts. They'll be so relieved it's manhoods not livelihoods, they won't see your razor coming.
ABRAHAM:	I don't know. My guys are fond of a paddle in the Red Sea. That's pretty salty...
ANAESTHETIST:	Trust me. In years to come, when youths are terrorising shopping centres, people will wish all hoodies had been cut off at birth. Now before you go sleepytime for these glimpses of the future, take this. (HANDS HIM A PRESCRIPTION).
ABRAHAM:	'You may feel drowsy for some time afterwards. Please sacrifice a three-year-old heifer, a three-year-old she-goat, a three-year-old ram, a young pigeon and a turtledove.'
ANAESTHETIST:	Any age. Not fussy.
ABRAHAM:	Fine by me. I'll do this sacrifice, as a reminder that there by the grace of You go I. You're good enough to grant me this fantastic land, and apparently all this offspring, although I'll believe it when I—

68

ANAESTHETIST: Night night.
ABRAHAM: Zzzzzzzzzzzzz...

A B E TV

*And like certain parts of Abraham, that show cuts
off there.
Now let's go back to Jeremiah Kyle, to see if
Abraham finally gets that son he's been talking
about. Yes, it's everyone's favourite episode:
The Paternity Test.*

The Jeremiah Kyle Show
Part two

KYLE   If you've just joined us, Abram and Sarai are
            here.
ABRAHAM   It's Abraham and Sarah, now.
KYLE   We'll change the caption.
            Now let's welcome Sarah's handmaiden Hagar
            to the show!

HAGAR ENTERS AND SITS.
CROWD DOESN'T KNOW
WHETHER TO CHEER OR BOO,
SO APPLAUDS POLITELY.

KYLE   Take a seat, Hagar. Nice to see your boss again?

HAGAR   She's no boss of mine. I quit. I don't need to work for her – I got a kid by her man.

CROWD OOH.

KYLE   Abraham? A kid by you? Let's get the paternity test ready.

ABRAHAM   No need, she's right, she's had a boy, Ishmael, and I'm the dad.

KYLE   Sarah? Wanna see the paternity test? Bet you need proof.

SARAH   No, Jeremy. I gave them both permission. I said if I can't give him a child, why doesn't he try with Hagar? There's a Promised Land at stake!

KYLE   Well, I've got the envelope now. Let's see. There's dramatic tension in the room.

ABRAHAM   No tension.

KYLE   Everyone's excited...

ABRAHAM   No one's excited. We all know. Ishmael's mine.

KYLE   (OPENING ENVELOPE) Ishmael's yours! I said it first.

More from Jeremiah and his guests later. Right now, let's see what's cooking with Abraham and Lot, and is that smoke coming from those cities? It can only be...

SODOM & GOMDINEWITHME

Three houses! Three dinner parties! One winner!
Everyone votes and has a right old good time of it.
Except the residents of Sodom and Gomorrah.

HOST 1
Abraham's Prediction Party and
Haggling Bonanza

First host is Abraham. He's welcoming three of the most
angelic angels, sent by the Lord but disguising their wings.
What's that under your coats, chaps? Abe welcomes
them in, fetches a calf, and dresses it.

Undressed Calf   *Dressed Calf*

Sarah's the hostess with the mostest, and one of the
angels shows off his prediction act by guessing her name,
then telling her she'll have a child – yes, in her eighties!
Sarah cackles away and the visiting angel tells her off for
thinking anything's too difficult for the Lord.

The angels are ready to rate Abe's hospitality ten out of ten, but a glance out of the window puts them right off their pudding. Our angels have seen the twin turbulent towns of Sodom and Gomorrah – well, you'll have plenty of time with Host 2 to check if it's best to just knock it down.

Abraham's concerned – Sodom is Lot's 'hood, and Abe's had enough of cutting off his family's hoods (see earlier covenant), so Abe ends the night with a fun haggling game:

'Would you destroy Sodom if there were fifty decent people in the city?'

'Weeelll, no, not if there were fifty,' replies God's angel.

'What about if there were forty-five upstanding folks there?'

'All right, forty-five good eggs in town, and they're safe as houses.'

The bidding war continues, till Abe pins down God to finding just ten nice people within Sodom's walls. Let's hope nephew Lot has recruited nine others to the Lord's way, otherwise it's curtains for anyone with an SG postcode!

Taxi home and the angels rate Abe's do 8/10. Or what about 7? All right, let's haggle down to 6...

HOST 2
Lot's do: Home Alone vs Straw Dogs vs War of the Worlds

Next up we're in Sodom, and Lot's the host! He welcomes the angels in, but uh-oh: some of the townsfolk look like they wanted an invite too. Lot's got his work cut out trying to keep them away. Don't spend all your time at the front door, Lot, you've a lasagne in the oven!

Looks like the locals want some hanky-panky with Lot's visiting angels. What a fine host Lot is though! He blocks the door and even offers his virginal daughters to the rampant mob. He's on target for a 10/10 vote for hospitality, although only 2/10 for parenting skills, and that's generous.

The angels step in with a blinding act – removing the eyesight of the randy locals so they can't find a way in. They could have just removed their libido, but either/or.

What a fire and brimstone finale! This is a dinner party to remember and no mistaking. Looks like time's up for Sodom and Gomorrah. God would have spared it if there'd been ten good 'uns, but it's just Lot, his wife and his two daughters. Even their fiancés roundly mocked father-in-law-to-be Lot. Shame!

0/10 for your behaviour. Sorry chaps!

[Let's not forget that while 'sodomy' got its name from 'Sodom' (history has forgotten what 'gomorrahy' must have been), the townies' sin wasn't a few guys holding hands, but their raping, pillaging, hedonistic debasement, greed, injustice and generally self self self: self-love, self-obsession, self-serving selfishness, self-assessment tax returns, selfie Facebook photos... I don't know if they had a department store but it was probably Selfridges.]

HOST 3
Lot's Daughters' Cave Night

For the final party the angels usher Lot, his wife and their daughters Pixie and Parking (my guesses at their names) out of their Sodomicile. It's a fair trek to the cave and the angels hurry Lot's lot along their way, singing Oasis songs as they go...

'By now they should have somehow realised what they're not to do...'

'And all the lights that lead the way are blinding...'

'Some day there's Gomorrah, caught beneath the landslide, in a Champagne Supernova in the sky...'

'Don't look back at Sodom, you didn't hear me say...'

Sorry Mrs Lot, you couldn't resist. She's turned into a pillar of salt, like someone's just spilt a lot of red wine on the carpet.

Lot never even got to say his goodbyes. The last thing he said to her was probably something innocent like, 'Darling, you've got something on your back.'

Lot and his daughters arrive at the cave for the rest of the party, and the rest of their lives as far as they're concerned. There's wine a-plenty, just no men, apart from dad, so the daughters get him steaming drunk and play spin the bottle. The result? Two pregnancies, and Lot gets the sons he always dreamt of. Except they're also his grandsons, and they're brothers but also each others' uncles. 4/10 for the genes.

So Abraham wins this week's 'Sodom and Gomdinewithme', because this is AbeTV and besides, this story of Lot's sons/grandsons – Moab and Benammi – is only here because they'd go on to form the Moabites and the Ammonites, future neighbours to Abraham's Canaanites. So it's a way of saying we're all related and let's get along. Bob's your uncle, and so's your brother.

One more instalment from Jeremiah Kyle as we meet the next patriarch, and hear about a father–son trip you'll never forget...

The Jeremiah Kyle Show
Part three

KYLE   Welcome back to the final part. We're with Abraham and Sarah. So tell me Sarah, you had a kid when you were ninety?

SARAH   (Sarah laughs) Ha! Yeah I did! So we called him 'Isaac'. Means 'he laughs'.

KYLE   Yeah, well I've heard people say to me 'You suck', which means 'I didn't laugh'. So Ishmael was out on his ear when Isaac came along?

ABRAHAM   Isaac was the promised one. Well, God did remind me not to forget Ishmael, that he'd have a great nation too. But yes. We kicked him out with his mum Hagar, a bottle of water and a loaf of bread.

KYLE   You kicked them out?!

ABRAHAM   Yes, at Isaac's weaning party.

KYLE   You had a weaning party? A party to celebrate him no longer being breastfed?

ABRAHAM   All the rage in our times. Food, dancing, an abundant supply of milk.

KYLE   Well, let's meet the new kid on the block – welcome Isaac to the show!

ISAAC ENTERS AND SITS. CROWD
CHEERS FOR HIM. ABRAHAM AND
SARAH CHEER FOR HIM MORE. A BIT
TOO MUCH.

ISAAC   Hi Dad. Mum. Mr Kyle.

ABRAHAM   Love you son.

KYLE   Ah but *do* you? You nearly killed him, didn't you Abraham?

ABRAHAM   Oh, on God's orders. I knew you'd bring this up. The good Lord just thought we might benefit from a bit of father–son bonding time.

KYLE   Yeah, bonding your son to a rock before
            sacrificing him. Hey, didn't I read that the
            Islamic tradition has the Prophet Muhammad
            ascending to paradise centuries later from this
            very same rock?

ABRAHAM   Where did you read that?

KYLE   Different book. Sorry. Back to you Isaac.

ISAAC   Hey, in Dad's defence, he did say there'd be a
            sacrifice. I kept asking where the lamb was. He
            kept saying God would provide one. And so I
            marched on, singing as I strode, 'Fol-de-ree!
            Fol-de-rah! Fol-de-ree! Fol-de-ra-ha-ha-ha-
            ha...!'

ABRAHAM   I heard God's voice saying, 'Don't kill him yet,
            Abraham.' And I kept wondering how exactly
            I'm going to get as many descendants as stars
            in the sky if I I'm told to sacrifice the boy.

KYLE   I hear at the last minute an angel intervened?
            Like our bouncers on this show.

ABRAHAM   Yeah. Told me I'd proved I feared God, and
            then drew my attention to a ram in the bushes.

ISAAC   That was handy.

KYLE   You must have been relieved, Isaac.

ISAAC   Yeah. Relieved everywhere, I was. Wasn't the
            best father–son trip we've had, but it's probably
            the last. Three days' walk home – there were a
            lot of awkward silences.

SARAH   'You boys had a nice time?' I asked when they
            got in. Well, you could cut the atmosphere with

a ... Sorry, shouldn't bring it up.

KYLE   Well, listen, you guys have been great guests.
          Look after yourselves, and each other.

OVER CREDITS...

After this show was recorded, Sarah died and was
buried in a cave near Hebron, bought by Abraham,
the first bit of 'Promised Land' to be purchased.
Abe remarried a woman called Keturah and had six
more kids, which finished him off. Isaac and Ishmael
buried Dad in that same field with Sarah – one of
three mothers to his children, but his true love.

is now closing for the night.
Please stand for the National Anthem.

9

Kids! You Three! Stop Squabbling!

Abraham is the granddaddy of the Bible: core to these early tales and promises, and indeed to Western religion itself. While in earthly terms Old Abe was a father of two sons, he's also a father of three religions...

The back seat of the family car led to considerable bickering on holidays.

- *Judaism:* Abraham's eldest child, about 3,000 years old. Judaism grew big and strong, the front runner in monotheism, standing up to older religions with many gods. Yes, Judaism was grounded for a bit in Egypt. It mucked about with a golden calf when it was told not to. But Judaism grew up knowing the difference between right and wrong. Obedience was key. A real high achiever, Judaism studied and worked hard, always believing in being the favourite child, thanks to God's covenant with Daddy Abraham.

- *Christianity:* In historical terms, the middle child – born a thousand years or so after elder brother Judaism. Child number two always gets a few hand-me-downs from Child number one, and this was no exception: the whole concept of monotheism, the Hebrew Bible, and a few traditions it may later shake off. As second children often do, they particularly sought love and a personal relationship with their Heavenly Father. Achievement wouldn't cut it. Christianity's bond with the Almighty needed to be an unconditional love – not just with a parent but with a best friend.

They found that best friend in Jesus. Elder brother Judaism had a love–hate relationship with this new family friend, culminating in scenes of tears when Jesus – a friend like no other – seemed to have vanished overnight. He came back, of course, and it was then that Christianity really came of age.

This young religion took the family book and added to it with a heartfelt series of journal entries, lessons and letters: talk of mission and change. It also travelled more than its elder brother: firstly to Syria, Mesopotamia and Egypt, then throughout the Roman Empire and Europe. Today, the two siblings get on, well, better than they used to.

- *Islam:* The third religion of Abraham, born in Arabia six hundred years after Christianity. The youngest quickly grew strong, passing over the family book in favour of its own: the Qur'an. It had a favourite teacher: a prophet, Muhammad. And as so often when it comes to third children, there aren't quite so many pictures of him.

  Islam grew up away from its older siblings, excelling in education, founding universities, and having hare-brained inventions like coffee, parachutes and three-course dinners. All the while its paternal origins were never forgotten, and Islam still refers to *'Millat Ibrahim'* – 'Faith of Abraham'.

As the siblings grew up, they grew apart. Yet all three see God as the sole creator and source of wisdom and morality. All three know of God's special relationship with Abraham. So occasionally the brothers do engage again. After all, family's family.

10

Twins!

Abraham's last wish was for son Isaac to be wed to one of his own, back home. He asked his eldest servant Eliezer to place his hand under his boss's thigh, to swear the most oathiest of oaths. Even today if you ask someone to do that ... well, they'll look at you funny, but times have changed.

Eliezer trekked from the Promised Land to the Pre-Promised Land of Haran, Abraham's birthplace, and that's where we meet Rebekah. 'Saac and Beks would become a star couple of the Bible, and we've got an exclusive:

'Oh it was so romantic...' reminisces Rebekah, 39, in a charming summer gown (available from Dorotheah Perkins). 'I was filling up at the well, and I saw Eliezer with ten camels. He looked so thirsty. His camels too – some of them really had the hump.' She giggles at her joke.

'He told me that he'd asked God that the first person who helped him with water would be "the one". And I guess I was the first and friendliest girl there that day. The crazy thing is, my grandma is Abraham's sister-in-law, so it all links back. It's nice. Although family get-togethers are confusing – I never know if I'm talking to my great aunt, my mother-in-law, or both.'

Rebekah invited Eliezer to stay with her dad Bethuel and brother Laban that night, and there the deal was struck that she'd be married to Abraham's son Isaac. Yet she baulks at the idea that it was an arranged marriage.

'Oh no,' she beams. 'I left straight away, and as soon as we arrived days later, Isaac ran out to great me in the field and I knew.'

Now she's mum to twins, who are proving quite a handful. 'Well they always were – even in the womb!' But it wasn't easy. 'I couldn't conceive to begin with, but now God's blessed us with these two fine boys.' Twins are often common in IVF births, I say to Rebekah. 'Well, it wasn't IVF as such,' she replies. 'Unless IVF stands for Infant Via FatherGod. Infertility Void Finally. Something like that.'

(*Shalom!* Magazine hears they're working on **I**mmortal **V**isitation **F**ertilisation, but Bethlehem NHS Trust reports that won't be ready for a few hundred years yet, and spaces will be very limited.)

'My boys are great,' smiles Rebekah. 'Especially Jacob. You shouldn't have favourites. But you know. Isaac prefers Esau, so it levels out.'

I ask if their favouritism causes the kids to quarrel. 'Oh, they quarrelled long before we picked favourites. In my womb they fought like, as God put it, two different nations. At war. A dawn raid near my left kidney, a skirmish on two fronts by my spleen...' She winces.

So what was the birth like? 'They fell out.' I wince. 'Oh no, I mean with each other, straight away. Well God told me the elder would serve the younger, and it's almost like they heard too and started scrapping. The first boy out looked red and hairy, like an angry Scotsman. So we called him Hairball.' Hairball? 'Esau, in the local language.'

And his brother? 'Born a few seconds later. He was actually grabbing Hairball's heel, so we called him Grabby, aka Jacob.'

And how's new daddy Isaac taking to all this? 'Oh, just great. He's sixty now, and his sight's already starting to go, so he leaves the childcare to me. But we can both tell these boys are going to be quite a handful. Hairy Esau's always out and about, and Grabby Jacob, well, he's my little star. He's a crafty one though...'

11

Jacob's Crackers

One man's 'crafty' is another man's 'entrepreneur'. Because as Jacob and Esau grew up into nagging brothers, Jakey-Boy showed a knack for being quite the lovable conman...

Only Drools at Soup Courses
Jakey-Boy Part 1

...So that dipstick Esau comes in drooling from a day hawking hooky meat from the van. I'm tucking into my soup course and he wants a bit, so I say cushdy, bruv. But in return, I want your birthright. He who dares, eh, he who dares...

Now of course Esau never was the sharpest tool in the forest, so he starts giving it all 'I'm gonna die, Jakey-Boy! What good's a birthright to me if I'm keeled over all Hank Marvin!'

He didn't half lay it on! So we done a deal there and then: his birthright as the eldest, for my bread and lentil consommé. Bonnet de douche, bruv, bonnet de douche!

Dad lost the use of his mince pies. Which of course I used to my advantage – play it cool, Jake, play it cool. See, on his deathbed Dad called in my older bruv, asked him for a nice bit of venison, so when Esau ran down the caff, Mum overheard and got me to take Dad some goat meat from the fridge. Course, Esau's hairier than a monkey with a kiwi fruit, while my head's as smooth as my patter, so I grabbed Esau's coat off the peg and started doing his voice.

Dad fell for it, 'cos his senses were telling him different things:

- *SMELL: unwashed hair, smells like Esau, the mucky pup.*
- *SOUND: sounds like Jacob. Uh oh.*
- *SIGHT: blind as a bat. No score there.*
- *TASTE: goat meat's no venison. Maybe he's thinking it's me ...*
- *TOUCH: ... ha ha, nice big mane, he thinks it's Esau.*

Dad gave me his big blessing. Mange tout, mon père!
Esau got back from the caff just in time to miss out.
He still got a blessing, mind, but you snooze – you lose.

Jacob thinks it's best do a runner from his bruv, so when we have more from Jakey-Boy later on, true to form he'll be living with a new crafty relative, Uncle Laban. First, on his way to Laban's he stops at Haran. He sleeps, and dreams a dream you could almost put to music ...

JACOB'S LADDER TO HEAVEN

There's a Jacob who's been acting guilty as sin
And he's running a long way, to Haran.
When he gets there he knows, if he lays on some stones
With a dream he will see what he's here for.
Oooh, oooooh, and he's dreaming a ladder to heaven.

There's a stairway that goes, up to where, heaven
knows,
(And you know what I'm saying has two meanings).
There are angels that climb, and descend in a line,
Which just shows God and man can start meeting.
And oooh, it makes Jake wonder ...

God declares Jacob's clan will be vast as the sand
And they'll spread through the land like a spready thing.
In his dreams Jacob hears God's word calm all his fears
So he promises now to start tithing.

And ooooh, it makes him wonder ...

So Jacob says if God stands by him, then he'll try him
Which is not the way you'd talk to Him.
But Jacob starts to realise now, though it's a long road,
There's still time to change the path he's on.

Before he winds on down the road
Jake builds a pillar just for God.
And then 'cos circumstance allows
He takes some oil, starts to douse.
Calls it 'Bethel' – means 'God's house'.

From now he'll follow what God says
And try and follow in His ways
But Jake's a crafty little fool.
He'll be a rock, but will he roll?

... For now he's dreaming of this stairway, in Haran.

Jacob arrived at Uncle Laban's without much to his name: not
even any Jacob's Creek or Jacob's Crackers. But Laban let him
in, because he was nice, or because he was devious and cunning
and knew he could get twenty years' free labour out of his
nephew. And if that wasn't exhausting enough, thanks to him
Jacob would have thirteen kids by four different women. Yet
Jacob only wanted one: his true love, Rachel. But the outcome
is less Mills & Boon, and more Mills & Boon & Boon &
Boon & Boon...

Jacob and Rachel
(and Leah, her sister)
(oh, and Bilhah, Rachel's maid)
(oh, and Zilpah, Leah's maid, but that's definitely it)
... A Romantic Tale

Jacob, newest heartthrob in town, manfully wrenched the stone from the top of the well. He did not know from whence he had found that power. All he knew was that the woman before him was the most beautiful he'd seen.

'I'm Rachel,' the lady blushed.

'Jacob,' he breathed, sweat dripping down his arms.

'You'd like a drink?'

'Thanks.'

She coyly drew from the well. She had heard that watering-holes were the places to meet men, but it had never happened for her, till now. Without warning, Jacob kissed her, lifted his voice and wept. And Rachel knew this was the man for her. Embarrassed, she changed the subject to pastoral farming.

'The sheep are flocking to drink the water you've released. My father will be pleased.'

'Oh, these are your father's sheep? Uncle Laban? Then you're my cousin.'

'Well, only very distant,' Rachel was quick to add.

'Oh, yes,' assured Jacob. 'I'm your father's sister's son. We're only first cousins. It's all still fine.'

*

'The bigger problem,' murmured Laban over a welcoming supper, 'is that Rachel's older sister should be married off first.'

He spoke of Leah, who was pouring wine for her father and making eyes at the new bachelor. And what eyes she had. They were, well, they were Marty Feldman. All over the place.

Jacob smiled politely at Leah, then smiled winsomely at her beautiful sister Rachel. The suitor turned to their father. 'Don't get me wrong, Leah is a gem. She has an amazing personality. You know what, I think we could be really good firm friends. I see her more as a confidante, a real sturdy pal...'

'I'm right here, you know,' said Leah, and her father waved her across the room.

Laban beckoned Jacob closer and whispered, 'Seven years of labour, and you get Rachel.'

They shook hands, and Jacob's eyes met Rachel's, and one of Leah's.

To Jacob, the seven years' engagement seemed just a few days, so in love with his bride was he, and before he knew it, his veiled bride was standing next to him. Yes, she chose not to speak during the wedding ceremony apart from some mumbled vows, but that was her love holding her tongue. Yes, she seemed a couple of inches shorter than she used to be, but that was her love driving her into the ground. Yes, through the veil he could almost make out two wonky eyes, but love is blind, and love had blinded her, or at least made her a bit skew-whiff with emotion. It was definitely Rachel, his beautiful betrothed. (Leah's absence was explained by her suddenly being called away for an emergency last-minute cribbage tournament.)

Jacob kissed his bride, and they became lovers in the night. Passions soared, their bodies clung, in ways that, ooh, well it was quite personal and the details are probably best left just for them really. All you need to know is that it was very, very dark.

When the morning light glanced over the distant mountains, the lovers awoke. The man smiled as sunbeams danced over his wife's arm-hairs, at how it lit up her cheek sores, at how its first rays glinted on her left eye fixed on the horizon, and her right eye staring at him...

'You're not Rachel!' cottoned on the now-married man. Bleary eyes recognised cross-eyes. 'Leah!'

'Oh. Good morning, Jacob,' she said. 'Or should I call you "Mr Leah"?'

'No!' he boomed. 'Where's your sister? Tell me you've just snuck in.'

She could not. Jacob, who had fooled his blind dad into blessing the wrong son when eldest and youngest were swapped, was himself fooled, blinded by love, into marrying the wrong daughter when eldest and youngest were swapped. 'Oh, cruel irony!' he bellowed to the world.

'In my defence,' Leah added, 'it was all Dad's idea.'

His uncle/father-in-law's excuse was that round this way, the eldest daughter must be married off first, apparently even at the expense of hoodwinking the groom.

'Ah, but now she is married off,' Laban exclaimed with a glint in his eye, 'the younger one is up for grabs. So you can have Rachel too! For just seven more years of service.'

'Oh, for crying out loud ... Fourteen years for two wives? You get less for murder.'

'Not technically true – around here you get stoned.'

'Oh shush. All right, seven more years. It's a good job my love for Rachel is everlasting, isn't it?'

'Well,' said Laban with a wry smile. 'This is a good way of double-checking.'

In time, Jacob took Rachel as his second wife, this time probably peeking under the veil to make sure it wasn't Laban in disguise. It wasn't: it was Rachel. And Jacob and Rachel lived happily ever after, with Leah, her sister and his first wife, with her lovely personality, generally hanging around.

Jacob loved Rachel greatly, but she was unable to give him children, so for this he returned to his first wife in the next bedroom. God looked kindly on Leah, because, well, no one else would. Slowly yet reluctantly, Jacob held his first wife close – and nine months later she had a boy, Reuben.

Gently yet unenthusiastically, he clung to her – and she conceived another boy, Simeon.

Tenderly yet resentfully, he clasped her to him – and three-quarters of a year later, Levi appeared.

Softly yet apathetically, he bedded Leah – and after a pregnancy, out came Judah.

Rachel looked on at her sister these four years, her eyes full of envy, and symmetrical. She needed to be able to offer Jacob some offspring or he would spring off, so under the custom of the day, she proffered her maiden Bilhah in her place.

Jacob took a deep breath, and affectionately yet hesitantly, he embraced the lie-down stand-in – and after some outsourced labour, Dan appeared.

Sensitively yet nervously, he clinched the foxy proxy – and after subcontracted contractions, a sixth boy arrived, Naphtali.

Leah saw these two boys, at the same time, even though one was standing in front of her and one right round to her left, which was a good trick. She was filled with sororal jealousy, and pondered the best way to anchor Jacob to her marital bed. Eventually she realised what Jacob would want more than anything: a seventh child.

So lovingly yet desperately, she bonded with her husband – yet with no child-based outcome. Leah knew what she had to do. It had worked for her sister, so she too would offer her maiden's womb in place of hers.

Jacob looked at second wife Rachel, second wife's maid Bilhah and her two sons, first wife Leah and her four sons, and now first wife's maid Zilpah with her fluttering eyelashes, and said, 'Oh well, in for a penny.' As Jacob and Zilpah climbed the stairs to her room, they could just make out the sound of Laban laughing, and howling something about 'another year's free labour from him with every labour from them!' They didn't get it.

Amorously yet bewilderedly, Jacob clutched the adequate surrogate – and some time later, she had a lad, Gad.

Warmly yet wearily, he lay with Leah's laid-on maiden – till she was laden with baby, Asher.

It all got very tricky. Four women, eight boys, Jacob working all day in Laban's fields for no wages, and zero child benefit. At one point Rachel sold a night with Jacob to her sister Leah in exchange for some mandrakes. Jacob had no say in this. By this stage, he was just going where he was told. So diligently yet drowsily, he climbed into bed and fought sleep to be with his first wife again – and she bore him Issachar.

Obediently yet groggily, he reposed with Leah – causing a tenth son, Zebulun.

Dutifully yet sulkily, Jacob knew her, vaguely, from somewhere, oh that's right it's wife number one – and Leah gave birth to – what's this? – a girl. After ten boys, it was one heck of a trick, so mother went 'D'nah!' And so they called her Dinah.

Anyone else would stop there, now there's finally one of each gender (and nine others). But God remembered Rachel. Jacob did too, dimly – it was so easy to lose track. Lovingly yet exhaustedly, Jacob shared a night of passion/snoring with his original sweetheart, wife number two, Rachel – and finally she carried a child of her own, a boy called Joseph.

And Jacob rested, and he saw all that he had procreated, and he saw that they were a noisy brash bunch who'd be unwelcome in most family restaurants. Jacob's tribe would soon become their own tribes. For now they were Reuben, Simeon and Levi, Zebulun and Issachar, Asher and Dasher, Dancer and Prancer, Donner and Blitzen, Grumpy, Dopey, Sneezy, Greedy, Gluttony, Tinky-Winky, Dipsy, Cuthbert, Dibble and Grub. Jacob had no idea. He'd lost count and just wanted a nice sit-down, maybe a sleep, and maybe a dream about a ladder.

12

Pharaoh's Phrases

Hi, I'm Pharaoh! I'm busy having dreams – not about ladders but about cows and sheaves and running in treacle (but we all have that one, so let's not bother about that). More of me later, but I thought you'd like to know some of the phenomenal phrases that have their genesis in Genesis. It's time for Pharaoh's Phrases!

'Be fruitful and multiply' (1:22)
Before it was reinvented as a coarse way of telling someone where to go, this had thankfully far purer roots. It's God's way of kickstarting the planet; how typical of us to use it to be rude.

'Spare rib' (2:21)
Well, actually it's from the German *ribbesper*, for pork that's been cooked on a spear. Sorry.

'Forbidden fruit' (2:17)
The phrase isn't biblical; it was first used in 1663 in a book about Oliver Cromwell. But we get the idea. That first fruit – never once mentioned to be an apple – was forbidden. *Verboten. Interdit.* Although it was before Babel, so it was just forbidden. But in Hebrew.

'Am I my brother's keeper?' (4:9)
Not a very good one, no Cain.

'Adam's apple' (3:6)
The theory is that Adam ate the apple, it caught in his throat, and that's why it's called an Adam's apple. Eve didn't have one because she ... juiced hers? No, no, no, none of it in the Bible. Goes to show how several millennia of tittle-tattle can create a name for a thing.

'Dust to dust' (3:19)
'Dust thou art, and unto dust shalt thou return,' the King James Bible says. All right, cheer up everybody! Handily this is only 0.17 per cent of the way through the Bible; the other 99.83 per cent of the Bible helps explain what comes after the dust.

'Sweat of your brow' (3:19)
God's curse on man was that he was going to sweat for his food from now on. Just don't let it drip in.

'Olive branch' (8:11)
The original peace sign. Oh and doves too. That's why you get doves released at some weddings, and not pigeons (unless you use a cheap wedding supplier).

'The Land of Nod' (4:16)
In modern times to visit here means you're having a bit of a doze – we can thank *Gulliver's Travels* author Jonathan Swift for introducing that idea in 1885. But before that, it was simply where Cain went to build a city.

'Raising Cain' (4:11)
Adam and Eve raised Cain as a child, but this modern phrase, not in the Bible and dating from the late nineteenth century, literally means to call up the cursed spirit of that first killer, but more figuratively means to cause quite a commotion.

'Fire and brimstone' (19:24)
This normally refers to a style of preaching rather the town-smiting in the original story. Brimstone is sulphur – add fire, and any school chemistry student will tell you to watch your eyebrows. Add it to a whole city, have God as the lab technician, and I'd do what the teacher always advised: 'Come and stand behind me.'

'The fat of the land' (45:18)
The crème de la crème, the cream of the crop, the cat's pyjamas, the dog's ... well, you get the picture. Pharaoh gave Joseph the best bits. And The Prodigy gave the title to their 1997 collection of phat beats.

'East of Eden' (3:24)
Great movie, great book, but hey fact fans, the Bible came first.

'Forty days and forty nights' (7:4)
The original forty days and nights – before the Wilderness, before Lent, before the Josh Hartnett movie – were Noah's rainfall.

'Hungry like the wolf' (49:27)
Not word-for-word in Genesis, but we'll see Jacob's blessing for Benjamin has him peckish like a certain lupine mammal. I'm sure Duran Duran were Bible-literate.

'One flesh' (2:24)
Long before The Spice Girls sang of two paradoxically becoming one, Genesis got there first...

'Instruments of cruelty' (49:5)
Known to some as a World of Warcraft achievement level, but first it was part of Jacob's summary on two of his sons' violent behaviour.

'The White Stripes' (30:37)
Everyone's favourite garage punk pseudo-sibling duo named themselves after their surname and the stripes in their favourite sweet. But as we'll discover in the next chapter, the original white stripes were ones Jacob stripped from a tree to genetically engineer stripy cattle. Obvs.

'God forbid' (44:7)
The King James Bible has this twenty-four times, and it's in Wycliffe's 1380 Bible, or sometimes the equivalent 'Far be it from me'.

'As old as Methuselah' (5:27)
That phrase isn't used here, but the lifespan of that original Duracell Bunny is.

'Gave up the ghost' (25:8)
Many early English Bible translations had this phrase. In fact 25:8 has so many synonyms that it sounds like the start of The Parrot Sketch... We're told 'Abraham gave up the ghost ... died in a good old age, an old man, and full of years' ...bereft of life he rests in peace, he's snuffed it ... this is an ex-Abraham.

99

13

The State of Israel

With at least eighteen mouths to feed (thirteen kids, their four mothers, his own, let alone various servants and hangers-on), Jacob's time with Uncle Laban was drawing to a close. It would be the end of his apprenticeship as a man of God, and with a turning-point on the horizon – when he would actually wrestle with God – Jacob was soon to put his trickster days behind him. Now he'd only scam if scammed, so his Unc pushed him into one last ruse...

Only Sheep and Cattle
Jakey-Boy Part 2

I'd had enough of Uncle Laban and his war stories – time to pack the Robin Reliant. Unc started moaning, of course. 'What am I gonna do, no one to look after me and my land?' Sniffled into his beard, guilted me into working another six years for him before he'd give me some livestock to keep the brood afloat.

Course I had a deal to strike. 'Unc!' I said. 'How about I just pick out the speckled and spotty cows and the brown sheep, and take those with me?'

'Fine, boy!' the sneaky old codger replied, hiding all the spotty cows and brown sheep while he was talking. Well, you got to get up early in the morning to get one over Jakey-Boy, so I engaged in what they call some 'genetic engineering'.

I got some poplar branches – nothing to do with the Tube, although if you do go up the Poplar branch, I know a mate in East London who can sort you out some cheap stereos – and I put some white stripes on 'em. The branches, not the stereos, I haven't got any White Stripes.

So he who dares... I put some branches where the cows was drinking, and you know someone's smiling down on me, 'cos before you could say 'fromage frais', the cows are having speckled calves, I've got a bumper crop of genetically engineered livestock, and Laban's doing his nut. Hyah hyah! So you know, he bent the rules, I bent the rules, and this time next year, I'll have a million cows.

Ye gods

Off we trot to Canaan, you know it makes sense. Didn't tell Laban 'cos he wanted yours truly to work for nothing for a few more years.

Then my cherub of a wife Rachel (or Raquel, as I call her) went and half-inched her old man's household idols – you know, these little pagan images, looked like something out of Peckham Market, but he loved 'em like his own flesh and blood.

I didn't even know she'd nicked 'em, till Uncle Laban caught up with us yelling about how his gods had gone missing. Now I may be a geezer but I'm no thief. So I told Unc that there's no way any of us have got 'em, and that if he finds them on any of our lot, he's got carte blanche to wring his neck.

Well, how was I supposed to know Raquel had 'em stuffed under her drawers? Well, she's a smart girl, she thought on her feet. Her dad was about to search her, so she starts with, 'The time of woman is upon me!' Nicely blagged, my darling! Nothing scares us blokes more than time of the month. Unc looked all embarrassed. Didn't even think to shake her down for his stolen wossnames.

Anyway, Uncle Laban and I thought best we call it a day there, so we shook hands, said pot pourri, and I never saw the old duffer again. Just one of my old muckers left to make peace with: and that's a certain plonker I once knew. Some call him Dave. I call him Esau.

Enough of the wheeler-dealer – Jacob puts that behind him now. He'd struck a deal with God that if He stuck by him, he would stick by Him, and God has more than delivered. Jacob has family, wealth, and now a chance to face his brother. Evolving from conman into holy man, right now he's got unfinished business...

THIS IS THE
Canaan Wrestling Federation

You join us live for the grudge match we all want to see: it's Grabber Jacob vs Esau the Hairy!

Esau the Wronged, it should be, Frank. These brothers have got scores to settle!

Right on, JJ. And here's Jacob, backed by his harem of wives, maidens and kids. He is the picture of the travelling family man.

And here comes his opponent Esau – it's a Big Brother Showdown!

Look at Esau flanked by four hundred men!

I would not want to be in Jacob's sandals right now, Frank.

We'll bring you all the action here on CWF, it's the Jacob vs Esau grudge match – but first, what's this?

Whoa, we have got a guest wrestler coming out to the ring now, and Jacob was not expecting this!

None of us thought we'd see this: new wrestler Angel, straight from the heavens, and it is on! Jacob and Angel are in the ring, and Angel has gone straight for a stranglehold!

Whoa, but Grabber Jacob is living up to his name by turning out into a bodylock! He is out here alone and wrestling with God.

He's got Angel against the ropes but Angel is not going to take that for long, and slamdown for Jacob! Jacob is on the mat – 1, 2... But he's up again!

SOME TIME LATER

This match now enters its tenth hour, JJ. JJ?

Huh? Wassat, Frank? What did I miss? Frank?

The last eight hours of wrestling, JJ. Now you take over, I'm going to sleep.

Wait! Look at this! Angel has just jabbed Grabber Jacob's hip joint, and Jacob does not like that. Look at the guy!

Jacob's hobbling around that ring like he's trodden on a plug.

What's a plug, Frank?

No idea, JJ, but look – Jacob's thigh's out of joint from that one touch! I have never seen anything like this. What are your predictions, JJ?

Well, Frank, I wouldn't be surprised if from this day on the Hebrews refrain from eating the sinew of hip in tribute to this very moment. But hey, I'm just a commentator.

I meant about the match, JJ.

Oh. Angel to win.

But it's not over yet. Jacob is grabbing Angel and he is not letting go until – did I hear that right? – until he blesses him? And he has! Angel has blessed Jacob! And Angel has given Jacob a new name: Israel!

I can really see that rebranding catching on with the fans.

Now Angel and Jacob – sorry, Israel – are shaking hands and both raising hands in victory. What a match, JJ.

And let's not forget this is all build-up to the big brother showdown: Jacob vs Esau.

That's Israel, JJ. He's now splashing his face and dividing his family. He's got the maidens Bilhah and Zilpah with their kids up front against Esau's men, then Leah and her kids, and saving favourite wife and son Rachel and Joseph right near the back. And that's got to hurt, JJ.

You're not wrong, Frank. Bilhah, Zilpah and to some extent Leah must be floored by that move.

And hold that thought, JJ – here comes Esau! And the crowd have gone wild! As he takes the ring now, a nervous Israel joins him, and seconds out and ... Israel's thrown some sheep his way!

He really wants to send Esau a message, and that message is: 'Here are some sheep.'

Looks like a gesture of peace and repentance to me, JJ, but Esau is sending them back, he doesn't want them. Instead Esau approaches Israel and – he's hugging Israel! This man of vengeance is just giving his brother a good old hug. JJ? Shall we hug it out too?

Yeah, all right. You're great, mate.

You too, old chum.

The Further Adventures of Jacob's Thirteen

LEAH's first four:

REUBEN was the eldest son, and really quite the lad.
He modelled everything he did on Jacob, his old dad.
But Reuben should have drawn the line when seeking out a lover,
Because he lay with Bilhah, Daddy's maid, his own stepmother.

SIMEON, the strongest son, is known for hating Joseph.
He envied his young brother and he didn't care who knows it.
'Twas him that pushed young Joseph into quite a scary pit,
And him that Joe held hostage, as we'll find out in a bit.

Pious LEVI's genes ensured he fathered priestly sons.
(That's 'Levi's genes' not 'Levi's jeans' – not denim 501s.)
His great-grandson was known, the book of Exodus discloses,
For parting seas and scaring Pharaoh: you'll know him as Moses.

Onan (JUDAH's son) took Tamar (his late brother's wife),
But failed the deed, and spilled his seed, so God took Onan's life.
Judah banished Tamar, who returned disguised and lured,
Gave birth to twins, and thus ensured that Jesus' line endured.

BILHAH (Rachel's maid)'s two:

DAN, the black sheep of the clan, was rather cruel and vicious.
Though good old Samson was of Dan, most others were malicious.
When Joseph's brothers bloodied dreamcoat, 'twas on Dan's advice,
And early Christians feared his tribe might spawn the Antichrist.

NAPHTALI, of Bilhah's kids, was certainly the littler.
Oddly his name means the same as that first book by Hitler.
You read that right – this trivia just takes a mental juggle:
'Naphtali' and 'Mein Kampf' both translate to mean 'My struggle'.

ZILPAH (Leah's maid)'s two:

GAD, among his brothers, really struggled to belong,
Perhaps because he grew up just a bit too big and strong.

His tribe were restless, first to exit Canaan, up and out,
So generally through history, he was the Gad-about.

ASHER, quite the peace-maker, was known for having boys,
Whose daughters were quite beautiful and elegant of poise.
His tribe struck oil, it's said, so they all ended up quite wealthy,
Although the oil was olive, so moreso they were quite healthy.

LEAH's next three:

ISSACHAR's a brilliant name, like Rufus, Geoff or Bernard,
And his descendants were, it's said, exceptionally learned.
Zebulun looked out for them, as their financial buddy,
To bankroll Issacharians to study, study, study.

Wealthy merchants were Zeb's tribe, so they did all the earning,
While next-door tribe of Issachar did all the godly learning.
They shared divine rewards, or so was hoped by ZEBULUN,
Who died himself in Sidon in the land of Lebanon.

DINAH went to Shechem, was defiled by their duke.
So brothers Si and Levi sought to savagely rebuke.
'Go circumcise yourself and all your men!' the brothers said.
With men still sore, the brothers roared and painted that town red...***

***(...But what's it really all about?
Well, they put swords in, they pulled swords out,
In, out, in, out, Shechem all about.
Told off by Jakey, 'Okay, Now you turn about.'
That's what it's all about.)

107

RACHEL's two (in reverse order):

The curious case of BENJAMIN is he's the youngest son,
And Jacob's second favourite child (Joseph's number one).
His mother sadly passed soon after hearing his first cooing,
And yes his name's the answer to 'Bob Marley, what you doing?'

JOSEPH was the favourite son – his brothers couldn't hack it,
Notably when Dad gave him this fancy coloured jacket.
He dreamed of bowing sheaves and stars; we now know what that
*   meant is*
Some time later Joseph would become...

14

Pharaoh's Apprentice

Twelve brothers. One dream job. One Pharaoh in need of the right business plan.

First, the tough talking...

REUBEN: As the firstborn of thirteen, I'm literally
            born to lead.

ASHER: I thrive to survive. In the boardroom, they
            call me Asher the Thrasher.

JUDAH: Like my great-great-great-great-great
            grandson Boaz before he meets his wife, I'm
            Ruthless.

JOSEPH: I may be one of the youngest in this process,
            but I'm a man with a dream, and that dream
            is that my brothers bow down to me.

Then, Dad tells them he means business...

JACOB: All right, enough chitchat. Joseph – I expect
            you're not exactly Mr Popular with your
            brothers, saying things like that.

JOSEPH:	I just say it like I see it, Dad. And they've been skiving.
GAD:	Oh, thanks.
JACOB:	Right, well you had your reward last week Joseph, that nice coat. You other kids work a bit harder, see what you can earn yourselves. This week's task is all about feeding a flock of sheep in Shechem. When I was your age I was out doing hard graft in the field, so that's what you've got to learn. You sort out your own Team Leader.

On the task and in the field, the boys decide who'll be Head Shepherd...

JOSEPH:	Well, I think I should be Head Shepherd because I had this dream where...
SIMEON:	Can we just put it to the vote – who thinks we should rip Joseph's coat off and shove him in a pit?
DAN:	Joseph? You're fired.
JOSEPH:	Thank you for this opportunity. Aaaaargh!

Joseph makes a pit-stop.

| REUBEN: | Guys! We'll fail the task if we actually kill him. Couldn't we just let him die of natural causes? |

JUDAH: Think good business sense. Let's sell him to those Ishmaelites as a slave.

But some passing Midianites have the same idea.

JOSEPH: (from the pit) The Midianites' pitch was very impressive, so I've decided to be sold to them. Bye!

REUBEN: Where's he gone?

The team split up: Joseph going to Egypt for the market research on slavery, the brothers returning to HQ to debrief.

GAD: I'm gutted we didn't get that big order from the Ishmaelites for one Joseph. We'd have something to show for this task apart from the coat we tore off his back.

DAN: It's all good, Gad. My background in graphic design means I just take his coloured coat, look – add some blood from a goat, and presto! It's only a prototype, but I'm confident this will convince in the boardroom.

Jacob, who started off deceiving his own dad using a goat and a coat (to seem hairy) is now being deceived by his own sons, using a goat and a coat.

BROTHERS: So what?

All right, don't have a go at the Narrator just because you don't get irony.

Back in the boardroom...

JACOB: What the blinking heck is this?! I wanted you to bring back a multicoloured coat with my boy in it, not some Butlins redcoat. Get back to the house, the lot of you. (*Sniffle*)

Week two: Egypt
There's a new boss looking for the perfect employee: The Captain of Pharaoh's Guard.

POTIPHAR: I'm impressed with what I've seen, Joseph. God's smiling on you. You're new, but I'm going to make you Team Leader in this house. For your household task, my associate Mrs Potiphar is going to shadow you, and she'll report back to me. Good luck, off you go.

MRS P: Joseph. What are you doing now?

JOSEPH: Is this for your notes?

MRS P: No, just for me. Let me help you off with your coat...

JOSEPH: Okay, well, I'm just going to focus on the task, the domestic chores.

MRS P: You can start with some jobs for me. I'd like
             you to turn down my room.

JOSEPH: With pleasure. I am definitely turning it
             down.

MRS P: I mean I want you in my bedroom, sorting
             the rumpled sheets.

JOSEPH: There aren't any rumpled sheets.

MRS P: Not yet.

JOSEPH: I'm out.

MRS P: Different show.

JOSEPH: I'm still out.

Back in the boardroom...

POTIPHAR: Mrs Potiphar, can you give me the results
             for Joseph on his household task?

MRS P: Not good, I'm afraid. He made an offer
             of himself, to me, but his pitch was not
             persuasive.

POTIPHAR: Did you make any orders?

MRS P: Yes, I told him to get out.

JOSEPH: With respect, that's not how it happened on
             the task.

POTIPHAR: With respect, button it. What's this, Mrs P?
             A bit of his coat?

MRS P: Yes, I kept it when he ran off after trying it
             on.

POTIPHAR: Wait, you tried his coat on?

MRS P: No, he tried it on.

POTIPHAR:	What's he trying his own coat on for?
MRS P:	No, he tried it on with me.
POTIPHAR:	You both tried it on?
MRS P:	Just him. Not the coat.
POTIPHAR:	Well, I'm confused.
JOSEPH:	It's twice now someone's taken the coat off my back. That's how good a salesman I am. And I didn't try it on with her.
POTIPHAR:	Right. The coat, or...?
JOE/MRS P:	No!
POTIPHAR:	All right, no need to shout. I'm only the flipping boss. Listen, it's decision time. Joseph – you've made a right pig's ear out of this. You come into my home, you start trying on coats with my wife. It's the end of the line for you. You're fired.

Joseph gets in the taxi and heads straight to prison.

Week Three: Prison
Potiphar's boss weighs in.

PHARAOH:	Good morning everyone.
JOSEPH/ BUTLER/ BAKER:	Good morning, Lord Pharaoh.
PHARAOH:	I'm going to mix the teams up a bit. My butler and baker failed last week's cooking task, so I want them to move over to Cell

Joseph. Joseph, you're new but I hear you're excelling as Project Manager in prison life. Keep it up. Any questions?

JOSEPH/
BUTLER/
BAKER: No, Lord Pharaoh.
PHARAOH: Good. See you on the next task.

The team, in pyjamas with a mug of cocoa, debrief on their dreams.

BUTLER: I dreamt about a vine, with like, three branches. And they were, like, well ripe. So I just, like, soooo pressed the grapes into, like, Lord Pharaoh's cup. And he was, like, 'Dude'. Do you know what I'm saying?
BAKER: Not really.
JOSEPH: Mmmhmm, mmmhmm, I see where you're coming from. Those three branches are three days. Lord Pharaoh's going to give you your job back. You'll be back in his Bentley and butling by the weekend!
BUTLER: I don't work weekends.
JOSEPH: Yeah all right, don't talk yourself out of a job. Just big me up to Lord Pharaoh when you're out, yeah?
BUTLER: Oh, totes bro, totes. I'm a team player.
BAKER: I just want to say, I appreciate you've had a dream experience, and that's great, but I too

have had some experience of dreaming. The other night there were three bread-baskets on my head, and these birds came down and ate them. So, you know, I'm clearly going all the way to the final boardroom too. Just sayin'.

JOSEPH: Ah, well that dream means you're birdmeat. Three days, you'll be in a taxi heading straight for the firing squad.

BAKER: I'd like to call a vote of no confidence in our Project Manager Joseph.

Three days later, and the final three are in the boardroom.

PHARAOH: Mr Bun the Baker. Why should I employ you in my organisation?

BAKER: Because...

PHARAOH: I don't want to hear it. You're leaving this process. You're ready-aim-fired.

BAKER: Thank you for the opportunity, Lord Pharaoh.

PHARAOH: Mr Butle the Butler. Why should I employ you in my organisation?

BUTLER: Because...

PHARAOH: I've heard enough. I like you. You're hired. I need a butler. Don't know how I've coped the last three days without one. The rest of you – that's you, Joseph – go back to the prison.

*Back in prison, two years pass.
And the Butler? Doesn't say a word about Joseph to
Lord Pharaoh.*

JOSEPH: I hate you, Butler.

7am...

SECRETARY: This is Lord Pharaoh's office. He would like
            to meet you at his Palace. The chariot will
            be with you in fifteen minutes.

*Some hairdrying, preening and suitcase-packing,
then...*

SECRETARY: Lord Pharaoh will see you now.
PHARAOH: Joseph, let's look at your CV. Sold to
            Ishmaelites. Wound up in Potiphar's house.
            Wound up Potiphar. Tried on his coat or
            something?
JOSEPH: No, that was a bit of miscommunication...
PHARAOH: I'm talking. So then prison, where according
            to my butler, you've been doing all right in
            the dream interpreting market. Well, let me
            tell you, interpreting dreams is big business.
            So in this task, I need you to tell me what's
            going on in my head.
JOSEPH: I think you'll find interpretations belong to
            God.

PHARAOH: Potato, potarto. What do you make of
                 this? There's me, at the Nile, and seven
                 fat cows come out, followed by seven thin
                 cows who eat the fat ones. Then there are
                 seven ears of corn, and seven thin ones
                 grow up and do in the first ones. What
                 does that mean? I'm thinking corporate
                 takeover.

JOSEPH: I believe you should expect seven years of
                 economic boom, followed by seven years of
                 deep recession and famine.

PHARAOH: Oh right, we got the economic forecast from
                 you now, have we? I should turn off my
                 Bloomberg and BBC Business Report and
                 just listen to you then, eh?

JOSEPH: Well, I'd just appoint your finest employee
                 to plan for this economic shift. If you see
                 my fifty-page business plan, I've proposed
                 storing a fifth of all produce, investing
                 profits securely in long-term bonds, and so
                 on ... I would be grateful if you'd pass this
                 onto whoever you choose.

PHARAOH: Joseph, you're hired! You are my new
                 business partner.

JOSEPH: Me? You must have got better qualified
                 people...

PHARAOH: No, you're my guy. As a reward, I'm going
                 to give you a wife, Asenath, daughter of
                 Potipherah, priest of On. You go off, have a

lovely time, then we'll get to business ready for this famine.

JOSEPH: Thank you, Lord Pharaoh.

PHARAOH: And I'm going to give you a new name.

JOSEPH: Ah! Like my father. His name was changed by God, from Jacob to Israel. Or my great-granddad – God changed him from Abram to Abraham. What am I to become?

PHARAOH: Zaphnathpaaneah.

JOSEPH: Yeah, God does it better.

Seven years of boom-time later, and apart from Pharaoh, Joseph is top dog in Egypt. The top dog has a couple of top puppies: Manasseh and Ephraim. Then the famine starts. Meanwhile, back in Canaan...

JACOB: Sons, fetch your passports. I'm sending you to Egypt.

BROTHERS: Yes!

JACOB: ...Because we've run out of food.

BROTHERS: Oh, yes.

After their journey...

SECRETARY: Zaphnathpaaneah will see you now.

ZEBULUN: Strange name.

ISSACHAR: You can talk, Zebulun.

ZEBULUN: Says you, Issachar...

REUBEN: Ssh! Show some respect, we've got to bow.

The candidates bow to their new boss.

JOSEPH: Reminds me of a dream I once had...

LEVI: What did he say?

NAPHTALI: I dunno. I don't speak Egyptian.

JOSEPH: Good morning. Now, who's missing?
    Someone not get out of bed this morning?

SIMEON: That's all ten of us. There are two other
    brothers, but Joseph fell in a pit a decade
    back, and Benjamin's at home with Dad and
    no food.

REUBEN: Simeon! Ssh!

JOSEPH: I don't buy it. This is corporate espionage!
    No one pulls the wool over the eyes of
    Zafthnafthpan ... Zathnafpanf ... No one
    fools Big Z.

GAD: No, we're brothers, promise! We're here for
    the right reason: some of your fine Egyptian
    cuisine. The famine's struck hard and our
    poor Dad...

JOSEPH: How is he?

GAD: Oh, fine. Just getting peckish.

JOSEPH: Tell you what, here's a task for you. Come
    back here with your other brother Benji,
    then I'll believe you. I'll give you three days
    in prison to think about it.

Talking time over, it's off to the prison...

REUBEN: I told you, we should have looked after Joseph.

SECRETARY: This is Zaphnathpaaneah's secretary. He would like Simeon to remain in prison. The rest of you are to fetch your younger brother. The taxis will be with you in twenty minutes. Please pack your overnight bags, where you'll find some corn and money as a gift.

Back in Canaan...

JUDAH: So we need to take Benjamin with us.

JACOB: But he's my favourite! (To Judah) No offence. (To Issachar) And no offence. (To Reuben) And to you. (To Asher) The same to you. (To Dan) And no offence to you. (To Gad) Nor to you. (To Zebulun) And no offence meant. (To Naphtali) And no offence, son. (Stares at Levi, then) What's up, Levi.

REUBEN: Dad, you can slay my two sons if we don't bring Benji back in one piece.

JACOB: I'm not sure I'll get over fatherly grief by slaying two of my grandchildren, but okay. Why did you tell him you had another brother?!

JUDAH:	Look, we'd better do it. We're hungry here.
JACOB:	All right then. Just take some gifts for this Zaphnathpaaneah fella. Here, a nice fruit basket. Some of these nuts. Some honey. A few of these nice spices.
LEVI:	Or we could just eat all that.

So back in Egypt...

JOSEPH:	Welcome back to the boardroom. Benjamin, nice of you to join us.
BENJAMIN:	Thank you, Mr Zaphnathpaaneah.
JOSEPH:	Have the comfy seat, Benjamin. Anything you need, you say.
DAN:	Speaking of seats, I've got to ask, Mr Zaphnath. You've seated us all in birth order? That's impressive.
JOSEPH:	Well, that's me. Now, for your final task: empty out your pockets.
ASHER:	What?
JOSEPH:	Don't ask, just do it. Someone's nicked my favourite mug.
GAD:	Well, it wasn't any of us. If you find it on any of us, honestly, you can kill him and the rest of us will be your slaves for ever.
REUBEN:	Ssssh! Why do you lot have to keep opening your big mouths?
JOSEPH:	Don't fret, I'll just take the culprit as a slave. Oh Benjamin? Your pocket's looking a little

mug-shaped.

BENJAMIN: What? It wasn't me! I don't even drink out of a mug!

LEVI: He's the youngest. He's got a sippy beaker.

JUDAH: Let me take his place. I'll be your slave. Let Benj go. Dad'll do his nut.

BROTHERS: Please!

JOSEPH: Enough! Right, crunch time. After a lot of deliberation, I have to say ... I'm Joseph.

NAPHTALI: What?

JOSEPH: Joseph. Your brother. In a pit. Ten-plus years ago. I've aged a bit, grown a beard, learnt Egyptian. Da-na. It's me.

LEVI: Why you little...

REUBEN: Hey! He's still number two man in all of Egypt.

JOSEPH: Exactly. And as for you lot... You're fed. And Dad too. Go get him, live here, eat as much as you like. What you lot meant for evil, God meant for good. So don't beat yourselves up, 'cos if you hadn't shoved me in a pit, I wouldn't have stored away a fifth of Egypt's produce for the last seven years. So with respect, you're f...orgiven.

Lord Pharaoh has found his apprentice, and his apprentice has found his family. So the brothers are given the fat of the land, not by The Prodigy, but by the prodigy, Joseph.

But back in Canaan, there's one more call, and it's from the biggest boss of all...

SECRETARY: Israel? Lord God would like to meet you at
Beersheba, where He met your dad Isaac
and granddad Abraham.

JACOB: Righto. I'll pack wood for an altar.

GOD: Jacob, I am God. The God of your father.
Do not fear what lies ahead in Egypt. I am
going to make a great nation of you. I'm
with you in Egypt, and always. I'll bring you
back, and when your time is up: trust me,
you'll have Joseph with you. Jacob: your
quest to find your son is at an end.

JOSEPH: Dad!

JACOB: Joseph!

JOSEPH: Call me Zafnafpanafzaf... Call me Joseph.

JACOB: Son!

And they make a life in Egypt – seventy in Jacob's family and household.
Aged 130, Israel blesses Pharaoh, but tougher times are ahead. With captivity, plagues and commandments will come a nastier Pharaoh: an Unpharaoh.
For now, Israel gathers his children, points his finger at each, and says ... You're blessed.

Epilogue
Jacob's Convalescing Blessing

The beginning of the end of the beginning of the Bible
Begins with Jacob's forecast for those twelve brothers tribal.
Reuben is the eldest, but forfeits firstborn blessing,
As he and Daddy's concubine were caught out while undressing.
Simeon and Levi avenged Israel's daughter
With 'instruments of cruelty' and circumcision-slaughter
So they bypass the blessing, and fourthborn Judah's first:
It's his sons who'll be kings, now the elder ones are cursed.
Zebulun shall settle by the sea and watch the waves.
Issachar's a strong old mule (becoming mostly slaves).
'Dan shall judge his people' and he'll be a snake that bridles
(His tribe become the judges, and they dabble with false idols).
A troop will conquer Gad, but in the long run he'll recapture.
Asher's land will yield fine bread that's practically focaccia.
'Naphtali gives goodly words' (his land is quite far-reaching.
So maybe this predicts that here's where Jesus starts
his teaching).
Benjamin is hungry like the wolf, so goes the song,
He may be young and small, but his tribe grow up
fierce and strong.

But Jacob's lasting message is to all the sons that tricked him:
Joseph's the most 'fruitful bough' – Blessed is the victim.

Then Joseph's sons were brought to Jacob: Gramps said,
'Bless the lads.'
And Joseph placed the eldest son by right hand of Granddad's.
The youngest was by Jacob's left, so he'd get second best,
But Jacob knew and crossed his hands, so youngest
was most blessed.

When aged the same as highest snooker break (that's 147)
Jacob died at last and climbed his ladder up to heaven.
Joseph vowed he'd bury Israel in the family tomb –
With Isaac, Abe, Rebekah, Sarah, Leah – if there's room.
And Joseph aged, his favourite coat soon faded grey and brown,
And he requested burial in his Egyptian town.
But Joseph knew one day they'd reach land promised
by God's word.
'So when you go, you pack my bones, make sure I'm reinterred.'
As Joseph dies, the book concludes: the end of the beginning.
We've seen creation, desolation, building, flooding, sinning,
And then the book got personal: covenants, vocations,
God and man's relationship grew down the generations.
Genesis has stirred the waves: up next, the seas will part.
We'll reach the Promised Land!
... And we've a promising head-start.

Suggested Further Reading

The Bible (especially the first bit.)

Also available by
Paul Kerensa:

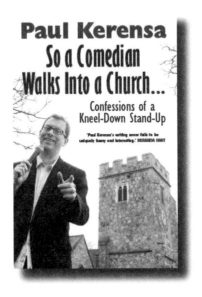

978-0-232-52979-1; Paperback; 198x126mm; £8.99

www.paulkerensa.com   @paulkerensa

And also from DLT Books: